D. Caroline Coile, Ph[...]

Chihuahuas

Everything about Purchase, Care, Nutrition,
Breeding, Behavior, and Training

With 45 Color Photographs

Illustrations by Michele Earle-Bridges

BARRON'S

All inquiries should be addressed to:
Barron's Educational Series, Inc.
250 Wireless Boulevard
Hauppauge, New York 11788

International Standard Book No. 0-8120-9345-3

Library of Congress Catalog Card No. 95-15009

Library of Congress Cataloging-in-Publication Data
Coile, D. Caroline.
    Chihuahuas : everything about purchase, care, nutrition, diseases, behavior, and breeding / D. Caroline Coile ; illustrations by Michele Earle-Bridges.
        p.   cm. — (A Complete pet owner's manual)
        Includes bibliographical references (p. 99) and index.
        ISBN 0-8120-9345-3
        1. Chihuahua dogs. I. Title. II. Series.
    SF429.C45C65   1995
    636.7'6—dc20   95-15009
                                                CIP
                                                AC

Printed in Hong Kong

13 12

About the Author

Caroline Coile is an award-winning author who has written articles about dogs for both scientific and lay publications. She holds a Ph.D. in the field of neuroscience and behavior, with special interests in canine sensory systems, genetics, and behavior. Her own dogs have been nationally ranked in conformation, obedience, and field-trial competition.

Photo Credits

Toni Tucker: inside back cover; Sandra Whittle and Cynda Seibert: front cover, pages 5, 16, 20 top and bottom, 32, 48, 56 top right, 61, 72, 76 bottom, 80 top and bottom, 81, 85, 89, inside front cover; Barbara Augello, back cover; Susan Green: pages 4, 21, 25, 45, 49, 52, 56 top left, 57, 65, 68, 69, 73, 92, 100 top; Lauren Lulich: page 9; Caroline Coile: pages 12, 33, 56 bottom, 64, 96 top and bottom, 100 bottom; Eileen Woliver: pages 13, 40; Robert DeJonge: page 37; Kathy Edwards: pages 41, 76 top, 93; Barbara M. Bonalski: pages 65, 84; Edith Varga Buchko: page 97.

Important Notes

This pet owner's guide tells the reader how to buy and care for a Chihuahua. The author and the publisher consider it important to point out that the advice given in the book is meant primarily for normally developed puppies from a good breeder—that is, dogs of excellent physical health and good character.

Anyone who adopts a fully grown dog should be aware that the animal has already formed its basic impressions of human beings. The new owner should watch the animal carefully, including its behavior toward humans, and should meet the previous owner. If the dog comes from a shelter, it may be possible to get some information on the dog's background and peculiarities there. There are dogs that, as a result of bad experiences with humans, behave in an unnatural manner or may even bite. Only people that have experience with dogs should take in such animals.

Caution is further advised in the association of children with dogs, in meeting with other dogs, and in exercising the dog without a leash.

Even well-behaved and carefully supervised dogs sometimes do damage to someone else's property or cause accidents. It is therefore in the owner's interest to be adequately insured against such eventualities, and we strongly urge all dog owners to purchase a liability policy that covers their dog.

Contents

Acknowledgments
The information contained in this book comes from a variety of sources: breeders, original research, scientific articles, veterinary journals, and a library of dog books. But by far my most heartfelt gratitude must go to my most demanding teachers, who have taught me the skills of both home repair and dog repair, allowed ample testing opportunities for behavioral problem cures, and whetted my curiosity (and carpets) about everything canine for the past twenty years: Baha, Khyber, Tundra, Kara, Hypatia, Savannah, Sissy, Dixie, Bobby, Kitty, Jeepers, Bean-Boy, Junior, KhaKha, Wolfman, and Stinky.

Chihuahuas are always ready for adventure.

The world's smallest dog enjoys immense popularity because of its beauty, intelligence, hardiness, and, most of all, its giant heart.

Preface

Everybody knows the Chihuahua, that pint-sized pup from south of the border. The smallest of all breeds, the Chihuahua boasts an enormous following. But there's more to a Chihuahua than your standard lapdog, and there's more—much more—involved in taking care of a Chihuahua than your average dog of any breed. Choosing, caring for, sheltering, and breeding the Chihuahua require special attention to details most dog owners never have to think about. Unfortunately, far too few Chihuahua owners think about them either—until it's too late.

Experienced Chihuahua breeders say they are haunted by stories of new puppy owners who never dreamed an accident would happen, who wish they had known earlier how to safeguard their charges. If one theme permeates this book, it is safety. Any dog is a big responsibility; a tiny dog is an enormous responsibility.

But readers of this book will gain more than safety tips. This is your invitation to meet the Chihuahua face-to-face, decide if it might be the breed for you, and if so, find the best possible Chihuahua available. Then, with your new Chihuahua firmly nestled in your lap, settle back for special tips on training, feeding, and living with a Chihuahua. Chapters on breed history and behavior will help you understand your friend a little better, and veterinary matters of importance to Chihuahuas will help you care for your friend a lot better. Whether you want to be the best owner ever, or have the best dog ever, I think you'll find something of value in the following pages.

Chihuahua owners describe their dogs as "almost human, capable even of crying human tears." There are some owners who consider this description as beneath the Chihuahua, however! The typical Chihuahua is equally at home guarding the yard against intruding birds, navigating a car trip across the country, directing the preparation of a meal, or monitoring the television from its owner's lap. Sweet and saucy, the Chihuahua personality sometimes seems contradictory; but that's because the Chihuahua is adaptable to fit with the many different lifestyles and personalities of people who have shared their lives with this remarkable breed.

The typical Chihuahua owner is a little old lady—and a brawny truck driver, a teenager, a movie star, a family of four—and maybe you?

D. Caroline Coile, Ph.D.

Aye, Chihuahua!

From a Mystic Past

Few breeds of dogs can claim as mystical or mysterious a past as can the Chihuahua—nor would want to. One of the very few native American breeds, the Chihuahua's roots trace back to the ancient Olmec, Toltec, and Aztec civilizations of Central America and Mexico. Exactly how they were developed, and the roles they played in the lives of these people, are questions to which the answers have long been lost. Still, research into these ancient cultures has led to some amazing, and sometimes appalling, aspects of the Chihuahua's roots.

Unlike most other cultures that eventually developed dog breeds, the early Americans had no large domesticated food animals. The Olmecs (now thought to be the mother culture of Mexico) trapped small animals, and occasionally hunted large animals, but it is unclear the role, if any, that dogs played in helping. The Olmecs did, however, have two sources of domesticated meat: turkeys and dogs. Although repulsive to modern Americans, this tradition of eating dogs was not unusual in early American civilizations.

By the age of the Toltecs, there is evidence that a plump, thick-necked little dog with short erect ears and tail was bred for the table, to be eaten principally by the nobility. Obviously this dog was not the Chihuahua as it is known today, but Toltec carvings dating from the ninth century A.D. show a small dog with rounded head and erect ears, clearly reminiscent of the Chihuahua. This dog, known as the

Techichi, is believed to be the ancestor of most Central American breeds, and was most fully developed by the conquerors of the Toltecs, the Aztecs.

The Aztecs kept several distinct types of dogs for a variety of purposes, including beasts of burden, wool producers, food, and yet another grim role: sacrificial animal. Aztec life was filled with attempts to ensure prosperity by appeasing the gods with ceremonial blood offerings, usually of captive humans. The ill-fated humans lived the life of kings until the fateful day, and it is likely that dogs destined for sacrifice may have been similarly

Chihuahuas are one of the few breeds considered indigenous to Mexico.

coddled. These dogs, preferably red or blue Techichis, lived in the temples of the priests, and no doubt filled the void when human prisoners were scarce. But why dogs?

Perhaps the answer lies in the mystical connotations associated with dogs, or at least these little dogs. Dogs were believed to be able to see into the future, and to cure disease by transferring sickness to other people. A small red dog was believed to guide the soul of the deceased to Mictlan, the underworld kingdom of the dead, helping the soul to cross the waters flowing between this world and the next. Such a dog was kept in every Aztec household and killed at the grave and buried with any family member who died. Archaeologists have found the Techichi, sometimes painted with vermilion, in human grave sites all over Mexico. Occasionally a pottery dog figurine was substituted for the real thing; such pottery figures and carvings were apparently also used for some mystic purpose in connection

Pottery resembling Chihuahuas has been found in Aztec graves.

with temple or home worship. Other accounts relate that dogs were burned together with the deceased in the belief that the sins of the human would be thus transferred to the dog. Why the dog was believed to have such powers is unclear; some believe it may have arisen through the ability of the dog to cure some aches by using it as a hot water bottle!

Of all of the cultures that have developed small dogs, the early Central Americans were the only ones to develop these dogs for means other than companionship. It is difficult to comprehend that people could have considered as a pet a dog that they used in sacrifice, burial rites, magic, medicine, and food, but some accounts contend that they were indeed pets as well. If so, it must have been a very different man-dog relationship than that which the modern Chihuahua enjoys with its family. Yet it must be understood that sacrifice was not considered an act of cruelty by these people, and it is conceivable that they considered that they were merely sending their pet along with its master or to live with the gods when they sacrificed it.

From Aztec to American

The Aztec civilization flourished until the coming of Hernando Cortés in the 1500s, when it came to an abrupt and ignoble ending. Unlike many of the Aztec treasures, the little Techichi seems to have aroused little fervor among the Spaniards, although a few were said to be brought back to Spain. Most, though, seem to have been for the most part abandoned. It is believed that these small dogs became feral, living off of birds, small rodents, and anything else they could eat in the mountains of Mexico. The Techichi was larger than today's Chihuahua, usually had long hair, and was said to be mute. Legend has it that it interbred

The long-coated variety makes an elegant addition to any home.

with prairie dogs, resulting in the breed's round head and flat tail, but this is clearly only legend.

But exactly how these dogs developed into the modern Chihuahua is unknown. Some authorities believe the Techichi was crossed with very small Asiatic hairless dogs brought into the region by migrating Indian tribes; others point to a more recent influence from the Manchester terrier. Others discount a Central American origin altogether, believing that the Chihuahua's roots lie in China.

At any rate, it was over three hundred more years until the dog now known as the Chihuahua made its appearance. In 1850, some very small dogs—some long haired, some short haired, and some even without hair— were discovered; the first two varieties were named Chihuahuas after the Mexican state in which they were found, and the hairless breed became the Mexican hairless. Still, the Chihuahua remained a rarity through the early 1900s, unknown even by the most devout dog aficionados of the day. Not until Xavier Cugat, "the rhumba king," was seen in the movies and later on his weekly television show with his cohort Chihuahuas, did the breed get widespread exposure. But that's all it took. Once the public got a glimpse of these mites from south of the border, the breed's rise in popularity was one of the most meteoric of any breed in American Kennel Club

(AKC) history, ultimately reaching its peak in 1964, when it was ranked third in AKC registrations among all breeds of dogs. The Chihuahua is split into two interbred varieties—smooth and long coated—both of which are the tiniest members of the Toy Group.

The Chihuahua's Chance

It's difficult to believe that such a fragile looking creature could descend from dogs forced to carry such a spiritual burden. No doubt it is this tough heritage that accounts for the tenacity and never-say-die attitude of the modern day Chihuahua. Today the Chihuahua is found around the world, fulfilling such roles as show dog, obedience competitor, tracking dog, hearing aid dog, and therapy dog. But whatever its job, the Chihuahua never forgets its primary role: that of loving companion. No longer worshipped by throngs from afar, it has adjusted quite well to life being worshipped by one family at a time.

Unfortunately, popularity has come at a dear price. Chihuahuas have been scandalously overbred, exploited by those who see them only as money-makers, and unwittingly abused by those who know no better. Serious lovers of the breed are fighting a battle against ignorance and apathy, which they know can only result in hereditary health problems, unwanted dogs, and broken hearts. The Chihuahua needs dedicated newcomers to become a part of its future, people who will nurture each baby throughout its life, and refrain from indiscriminate breeding. Will that be you?

Is the Chihuahua for You?

The Reality Check

Chihuahuas make wonderful pets in part because they are almost childlike in their dependence upon their human families, and because they bond so deeply with them. Don't get a Chihuahua on a trial basis. If you tire of your dog and think it won't be bothered when you cast it aside, think again. After you have used up its irresistibly cute puppy months, there will be few people lining up to offer it a new home.

It's easy to imagine yourself with a loving companion, warming your lap and shadowing your steps, providing love on lonely days and security on lonely nights. And these scenes are very much a part of living with a Chihuahua. But there are also scenes of soiled floors, midnight walks in the rain, and trips to the veterinarian. There is the daily absolute responsibility of feeding, exercising, and loving your Chihuahua, no matter what else is happening in your life. Getting a dog will involve some sacrifice from everyone in your home, whether it be losing a favorite shoe, a night's uninterrupted sleep, or the freedom to take a trip around the world.

There are costs: food, equipment, boarding, and veterinary bills can be high. Check the veterinary prices in your area for office visits, a series of puppy vaccinations, deworming, yearly checkups, neutering or spaying, emergency clinic visits, and monthly heartworm prevention. The small size of the Chihuahua does bring some smaller bills, but many other services cost as much as they would for a Great Dane.

Spend a moment contemplating just why you want a dog, and more specifically, a Chihuahua. Obviously if your list of priorities includes protection or hunting ability or jogging companionship, perhaps you should reconsider the Chihuahua as your first choice. Don't choose a Chihuahua because your neighbor has one, or just because it's small. Chihuahuas aren't the only small breed of dog. Every breed has its good and bad points, and different breeds are more suited to different people.

Temperament

A moment of reflection on the Chihuahua's tumultuous history and it is no small wonder that these are tough hardy little dogs. Chihuahuas are intelligent, attentive, and willing to please, a combination that makes for a very obedient companion. They flourish as watchdogs and lapdogs, protectors and protectees. They are fiercely loyal to their family, or more often, one family member. Saucy, spunky, lively, bold, and quick witted, Chihuahuas make active companions. But at the same time, they are cuddly, loving, and demonstrative, sometimes to the point of being clinging. Don't get a Chihuahua if you don't want a constant addition to your lap.

The Chihuahua's diminutive size is an asset, enabling it to accompany its family in many places where a larger dog would not be practical. A small dog eats less, messes less, sheds less, requires less exercise, and takes up less room. And it fits nicely on any size lap.

But the Chihuahua is no mere lap-dog. It is the prototypic big dog in a little package. It bonds closely with its family, and appoints itself as guardian. Woe to any intruder's ankles who dares to trespass without the resident Chihuahua's approval! Chihuahuas have been described as "clannish," bonding closely with Chihuahua housemates and joining together to protect their territory from non-Chihuahua canine intruders. The Chihuahua is a spunky chap that often astounds its owners with its fearless attitude in the face of adversity.

This attitude is not without its drawbacks, however. No matter what some Chihuahuas think, they are small dogs and vulnerable to serious injuries from accidents and assaults. Luckily, most Chihuahuas' feistiness does seem to be tempered by good sense. The watchdog attitude can be annoying to owners who cannot tolerate noise, because the Chihuahua is a gifted barker.

The Chihuahua is obviously not a breed to be kept outdoors. Not only is it physically unsuited to brave the elements, but this is a breed that demands to be close to its people at all times. Left outside, many will dig or bark.

Poorly bred Chihuahuas have given the breed a reputation for being snappy and high strung. Well-bred Chihuahuas are neither of these. True, they are not a good choice as a young child's pet, but this is mostly because they are too fragile to be safe with rowdy children, and may become intolerant if hurt. Some Chihuahuas can be shy, but most Chihuahuas that get out and about for socialization as youngsters grow up well adjusted. Chihuahuas are active, but not hyperactive.

Health and Longevity

Like most small dogs, Chihuahuas are long lived. The average life span is 12 years; many live into their teens, and some unusual individuals live into their twenties.

Chihuahuas tend to be extremely healthy, but it's easy to let some get overweight, especially females. Like many small dogs, they are prone to dislocation of the kneecap (patellar luxation), which can cause lameness. Serious cases can be corrected surgically. Collapsed tracheae are sometimes seen in older overweight dogs. The following conditions have also been reported with a somewhat higher frequency than in most other breeds:

Skeletal
• Patellar luxation (dislocation of the kneecap)
• Scapular luxation (dislocation of the shoulder)

The Chihuahua attracts attention wherever it goes because of its diminutive size and prancing gait.

With its courage and tenacity far outweighing its strength, this Chihuahua appears to nonetheless be winning a game of Tug O' War with its larger friend.

• Hypoplasia of dens (underdevelopment of the axis vertebra)

Circulatory
• Pulmonic stenosis (congenital narrowing of the outlet of a ventricle of the heart)
• Mitral valve defects (defects of the mitral valve of the heart)
• Hemophilia A (blood-clotting disorder)
• Factor VIII or AHF deficiency (deficiency of a blood-clotting factor)

Nervous
• Seizures
• Hydrocephalus (swelling of the brain)

Visual
• Secondary glaucoma (increased pressure within the eyeball)
• Corneal edema (swelling of the cornea)
• Iris atrophy (wasting away of the iris)
• Keratitis sicca (dry eye)

Miscellaneous
• Hypoglycemia (low blood sugar)
• Cleft palate (palate divided in two by a groove)
• Undescended testicle (a testicle that has not emerged into the scrotum)

Don't be alarmed by what may seem to be a long list of problems. All breeds of dogs have their own medical problems; more popular breeds have enough individuals seen at clinics for a trend to be discerned. Responsible breeders test all potential breeding stock, neutering those that are affected or that are shown to be carriers. However, the hereditary aspects, if any, of most of these conditions are unknown.

An open fontanel (molera) is common and not considered abnormal for the breed. Dogs with smaller, more domed heads are more likely to keep the open fontanel throughout life; in those with larger, less rounded heads, the opening will likely close by the time the dog reaches adulthood. Dogs with open fontanels require some

The molera, or open fontanel, is located on the Chihuahua in the same place as the soft spot is on a baby's head.

extra vigilance to ensure that they do not hit their heads in the open spot. Veterinarians who are not familiar with this normal Chihuahua trait have been known to mistakenly diagnose hydrocephalus in young puppies.

Their diminutive size makes Chihuahuas prone to accidents. Although their bones are strong for their size, they are small bones and as such can be easily broken. Chihuahuas are not a good choice for a home full of untamed children or heavy-footed adults.

Chihuahuas are not good cold weather dogs, and must be protected from the elements. Even long-haired Chihuahuas do not have the insulation necessary to prevent them from freezing to death in cold temperatures. Nor are they good hot weather dogs. It is simply a matter of physics that very small bodies do not tolerate any extremes of temperature well.

It is a wonder that a breed that has been bred down in size to the extent that the Chihuahua has is in general such a healthy breed. It is difficult to reduce size proportionally in all parts of an animal, including its organs; for example, the eyes of small dogs are proportionally larger than those of large dogs, often despite the best efforts of breeders to reduce eye size. This may explain why some of the very tiniest Chihuahuas are thought to be less hardy than the average size Chihuahua; perhaps some internal organs simply have their limits concerning size and normal function. Again, very small bodies don't have the energy reserves in store that larger bodies do and may be more vulnerable to food deprivation or minor illness that would not bother most larger dogs.

More the merrier?: There are certain advantages, and disadvantages, to having more than one dog. Two dogs are twice the fun of one, without being twice the work. Consider adding another pet if you are gone for most of the day. Chihuahuas love to cuddle with each other, and generally get along well. A cat, too, can be a good companion. For obvious safety reasons, a large dog is not a good match.

When introducing new dogs, it is best if both are taken to a neutral site so that territoriality does not provoke aggression. Two people walking the dogs beside each other as they would on a regular walk is an ideal way for dogs to accept each other. If you are introducing a new animal, give your original dog extra attention and perhaps extra tidbits in the presence of the newcomer so that it does not become jealous.

Warning: Chihuahua ownership may be addictive. Chihuahua owners have a tendency to go overboard, and fill their homes with Chihuahuas in every nook and cranny. Just be sure you have enough time to dote on each and every one!

Finding the Best Chihuahua for You

All Chihuahuas are special, but some are more special than others. You can find a Chihuahua today, but you can't find just the right Chihuahua in a day. Surely you can wait a little longer to locate the dog that will be a part of your family and life for the next 10 to 20 years.

Age: The age at which you bring your Chihuahua home depends upon its size, health, and maturity. Although most puppies are ideally brought home between 8 and 12 weeks of age, many breeders insist upon keeping smaller Chihuahua puppies until 12 to 16 weeks of age. This is because the very small puppies are more likely to succumb to minor illness if not treated immediately; as previously stated, small animals have little reserves to fall back on. If you definitely want a show-quality dog, you may have to wait until the pups are six months of age. No matter what the age, if the puppy has been properly socialized, your Chihuahua will soon blend into your family life and love you as though it has always owned you.

Although most prospective owners think in terms of getting a puppy, don't dismiss the idea of acquiring an older Chihuahua. No one can deny that a puppy is cute and fun, but a puppy is much like a baby; you can't ever be too busy to walk, feed, supervise, or clean. If you work or have limited patience or energy, consider an older puppy or adult because it won't require so much intensive care.

Sex: The choice of male versus female is largely one of personal preference, but keep the following pros and cons in mind:

Females are softer in expression and temperament than are males. There is not the size (or coat) difference seen in some other breeds between the sexes. They come in estrus twice a year; this lasts for three weeks, during which time you must contend with a slight bloody discharge and keep amorous neighborhood males at bay.

Males tend to be somewhat cockier than females. Unless neutered, they tend to become preoccupied with flirting with the females and sparring with the males. Some may also lift their legs in the house. Unneutered (intact) males, especially of the same age, are apt to engage in dominance disputes; intact females together have a slight tendency to scuffle as well. Intact males and females get along the best, but will provide you with the biyearly problem of keeping Romeo and Juliet separated. Most of the problems associated with either sex can be overcome by neutering, which is highly suggested.

Esthetics: Chihuahuas come in such an array of colors and patterns that you should be able to get just the color that most appeals to you. Try to see many different color Chihuahuas before committing to one. Blue- or gray-colored Chihuahuas tend to have more sparse coats, and may be more prone to some skin problems.

One of the innumerable advantages to being little is that shedding need not be a major consideration in choosing coat length. Many breeders believe that the long coat Chihuahuas are bolder and more gregarious than are the smooth coats, who tend to be more reserved.

Many people want the smallest Chihuahua they can get, the so-called "teacup" or "pocket-sized" Chihuahuas. As long as you are willing to take the extra safety responsibilities that such a tiny dog entails, these are indeed enchanting pets. You cannot breed the tiny females, however. And you must be more diligent with their health and feeding; very small dogs are more prone to hypoglycemia if meals are missed. They are also more susceptible to extremes of both heat and cold. Some breeders will charge more for the tiny sizes (although the Chihuahua Club of America does not endorse this practice), and some will not allow them to go to homes with small children.

Although these youngsters are enjoying a short romp in the snow, Chihuahuas must not be allowed to become chilled.

One esthetic choice that should be addressed is to what extent you want your Chihuahua to look like a Chihuahua. The one overwhelming hallmark of the Chihuahua is its tiny size. Yet it is not uncommon to see 10-pound (4.5 kg) dogs claiming to be Chihuahuas. Perhaps more than most breeds, pet-quality Chihuahuas simply do not look like Chihuahuas.

Chihuahua Choices and Chances

As you see more Chihuahuas, you will begin to notice that they don't all look alike, and the difference is more than just fur deep. All Chihuahuas are not created equal, and you will need to decide early on whether you are looking for pet, show, or breeding quality.

Pet: Although of course you want a dog that will be first and foremost a pet, in dog lingo, pet quality refers to a dog that has one or more traits that would make winning with it in the show ring difficult to impossible. These may include failure of the testicles to descend into the scrotum, cowhocks, or improper head profile, often faults that would never be evident to any but the most ardent Chihuahua fancier. All make beautiful pets. More severe flaws make a Chihuahua not look like a Chihuahua, such as having flop ears or being oversize. Beware of flaws that make the Chihuahua less than pet quality: flaws in temperament, such as shyness or aggressiveness, or in health.

Show: Show-quality dogs should first of all be pet quality. On top of this, they must conform closely to the Chihuahua standard of perfection so that they could compete in the show ring with a reasonable expectation of finishing a championship.

Breeding: Breeding-quality dogs come from impeccable backgrounds, and are of even higher show quality than are show-quality dogs. They have usually already achieved their championships. They have been tested to be free of hereditary health problems. If a female, she is large enough (over 4 pounds [1.8 kg]) to deliver puppies safely. Breeding quality means more than the ability to impregnate or conceive, but far too often these are the only criteria applied to prospective parents by owners unduly impressed by an AKC registration certificate. It is difficult to pick a show-quality puppy at an early age; it is impossible to pick a breeding-quality puppy.

Cost: Chihuahuas are not cheap dogs. A good pet costs from $250; show quality can run $500 to $1,000. Many people are surprised that a little dog costs so much, but there is no reason to expect that they should be priced by the pound. The small litter size, and often large litter expense (especially if a cesarean section is needed), accounts for the price tag of several hundred dollars for pet puppies. Show puppies and older puppies will cost more. Compared to the many years of companionship a healthy dog will give you, you will find that a good-quality Chihuahua is the deal of a lifetime!

Buyer Beware

Whether you want pet, show, or breeding quality, you must be very careful about where you find your Chihuahua. You want to avoid puppies from parents whose only claim to breeding quality is fertility. And you want to avoid buying from a breeder whose only claim to that title is owning a fertile Chihuahua.

You may think that if you only want pet quality you don't have to be so careful. But consider again the most important attributes of a pet: good health and good temperament. Many people mistakenly believe that the phrase "AKC registered" is an assurance of quality. But it can no more assure quality any more than the registration of your car is an assurance of automotive quality. Few people would buy a car from a stranger without extensive checking and testing, but many people answer the first ad they see in the paper and come home with a Chihuahua puppy about which they know nothing except that it is AKC registered. Chihuahuas seem particularly vulnerable to being exploited and foolishly bred. Puppies are sold at flea markets, through puppy mills, and in thousands of backyards throughout the country. They are bred by people who never heard of testing for hereditary health problems, and who don't even realize they are doing anything wrong. They are bred by people who neither care nor know about prenatal care and puppy socialization, and who have never even read the standard.

Buy the best dog, with the best parents, from the best breeder possible, even if you only want a pet. It is best if you can first see the parents and puppies, and if you get some type of guarantee. But a word of caution about guarantees from any source: no guarantee can reimburse you for your broken heart when your puppy dies. And replacement guarantees that require you to return the original dog aren't worth much when you already love that original dog.

HOW-TO:
Acquiring a Chihuahua

Some pros and cons of the more common sources for acquiring a Chihuahua follow:

Pet stores: Most pet stores can obtain any breed of dog within a short period of time. More importantly, however, a store should be able to provide the same information about a puppy's background that you would get directly from a breeder, such as the pedigrees and health records of the puppy's parents; whether the puppy was raised around people or in a cage; how long it stayed with the mother; and so forth. The store should also guarantee that it will take back the puppy if it becomes ill.

Newspaper advertisements: Chihuahuas can always be found for sale in the newspaper classified ads. Some ads are placed by knowledgeable breeders, but most are placed by naive backyard breeders. Cross

A good way to find a Chihuahua to purchase is to attend a dog show and talk to breeders.

When looking to purchase a Chihuahua, check the classified section of your local newspaper. Be careful which ads you answer, however, because not all are placed by responsible breeders.

out any ads that use the phrases "full-blooded," "thoroughbred," or "has papers" to denote purebred or registered, or "dame" to denote dam, because these are not terms that would be used by a knowledgeable breeder. Cross off any that say "ready by Christmas" because holidays are no excuse to get a puppy, and a pup should never be given as a surprise. Do not be impressed by claims of "many champions in background," because if these champions are more than two generations away they will have little influence on the quality of your pup. And if the main selling point is that the puppies have been wormed and vaccinated, then they must not have much going for them, because all pups of selling age should have been vaccinated. On the other hand, an ad that can boast of at least one parent being titled indicates that the breeder is

concerned with quality. Statements such as "raised with children," "health guarantee," or "breed information provided" hint that this breeder may be more knowledgeable than average and is willing to put effort into producing a healthy, well-socialized puppy. Such breeders might be worth a call.

Dog magazines: A quick way to contact several serious breeders is to look in the classified section of one of the monthly dog magazines available at larger newsstands. Even better is the current issue of *Los Chihuahuas* magazine (see Useful Addresses and Literature, page 99). The disadvantage is that if the breeder is located a distance from you, you will not be able to evaluate the dogs in the flesh, and you will not be able to choose your own puppy. Also, shipping adds an additional expense and can be stressful for an older puppy.

Dog shows: If at all possible, attend a dog show. You can contact the AKC for the date of a show in your area; these are also listed in *Dog World* magazine. Most shows start at 8 A.M., so unless you know when the Chihuahuas are being judged, you must get there early or risk missing them altogether. Tell the Chihuahua exhibitors of your interest and arrange to talk with several after they have finished in the show ring. Some dogs may be shown by professional dog handlers. Talk to them, too, because they will be able to give you a more unbiased view of the Chihuahua in comparison to the other breeds they show.

Why contact a show breeder if all you want is a pet? Because these breeders will have raised your pet as though it were their next Best in Show winner. It will have received the same pre-natal care, nutrition, and socialization as every prospective champion in that litter. And the breeder should be knowledgeable and conscientious enough to have also considered temperament and health when planning the breeding. If this is to be your first Chihuahua, then you will profit from continued advice from an experienced Chihuahua owner as your puppy grows. The serious hobby breeder is just a phone call away, and will be concerned that both you and the puppy are getting along well. In fact, because many breeders will expect to keep in touch with the owners of all of the puppies, whether pet or show,

Don't forget the local animal shelter when searching for a Chihuahua to join your family. You may rescue a pup in dire straits, while finding a lifetime friend.

throughout their lives, you may find yourself a member of an adopted extended family of sorts, all of whom are available for advice, help, consolation, and celebration. Finally, because in some sense the non-show puppy is a byproduct of the litter, most breeders are not out to make a buck from pet puppies, and prices are generally quite reasonable.

Breed clubs and rescue organizations: The Chihuahua Club of America (see Useful Addresses and Literature, page 99), as well as the regional Chihuahua clubs are an excellent source of reputable breeders. In addition, if you are interested in an older dog, ask to be put in contact with the breed rescue group, which finds homes for Chihuahuas that have fallen upon hard times.

Animal shelters: Sadly, not all Chihuahuas in trouble are fortunate enough to find their

way to a rescue organization. Some can be found in animal shelters, awaiting a new home before time runs out. But before giving your heart to such a cause, find out why that Chihuahua has been given up. Was it a lost dog? Did its former owner die, move, or become too infirm to care for it? Or does the dog have behavioral problems that would make it difficult for anyone to live with? If so, speak with a veterinarian, knowledgeable dog trainer, or behaviorist and ask what the treatment and prognosis is for that behavior. Don't allow somebody else's problem to become your heartache.

Although adopting a dog often means a lot of work, there is immense satisfaction in knowing that you are that dog's savior, and are offering it a life filled with love and understanding that it may never have experienced before.

The varieties of colors and coat types, each with its own special beauty, presents a prospective owner with some tough decisions.

The only thing that Chihuahuas like as much as cuddling with their owners is cuddling with each other.

Healthy pups are an appropriate weight, have clean and parasite-free coats, and exhibit the alert demeanor evident in these two youngsters.

Evaluating Breeders

If you have decided to contact a breeder, you should prepare a list of questions so that you can narrow the field further. "Why did you breed the litter?" (bad answers: money, friend wanted a puppy, always breed her); "How did you choose the sire?" (bad answers: convenience, always use him); "How do you screen for health problems?" (bad answer: what health problems?). Ask about the parents. Do they have conformation or obedience titles? This is not only important if you want a show/obedience prospect, but again, the answer can give you a clue about the care taken with the litter. What kind of temperaments do the parents and the puppies have? If some puppies are being sold as pet quality, why? Have the parents or puppies had any health problems?

Ask the breeder about the terms of sale. Don't fall in love with a puppy and then have to walk away because an agreement could not be reached. There are several possibilities, the easiest being that you will pay a set amount (usually cash) and receive full ownership. If registration papers cost extra, shy away. Sometimes concerned breeders will insist upon having a pet puppy neutered before supplying the papers, or they may stipulate that a pet puppy is to have a "limited registration," which means it cannot be shown or bred. Sometimes a breeder will insist upon co-owning the puppy. If the co-ownership obligates you to breed the dog in the future, go elsewhere. If the co-ownership is for insurance that the dog will be returned to the breeder in the event you cannot keep it, then such an agreement is acceptable. Any terms should be in writing.

Once you have narrowed down your list, if possible, arrange to visit the breeder. However large or small the operation, look for facilities that are clean and safe. Again, these are clues about the care given your prospective puppy. The adults should be clean, groomed, and in apparent good health. Look to the adults for the dog your puppy will become. If you don't care for their looks or temperaments, say good-bye.

Don't visit from one breeder to another on the same day, and certainly do not visit the animal shelter beforehand. Puppies are vulnerable to many deadly diseases that you can transmit by way of your hands, clothes, and shoes. Always go to view puppies prepared to leave without one if you don't see exactly what you want. This is not something you can trade in once you find a better one.

Hold the puppy securely, supporting it by the chest and hind legs, and resting it against your body.

Evaluating Puppies

Chihuahua puppies are fragile little beings, and you must be extremely careful where you step and how you handle them. Never pick up a puppy by its legs or head or tail; cradle the puppy with both hands, one under the body, the other around its side, so that the puppy is nestled securely against your chest. Keep a firm hold lest the pup try to jump out of your arms unexpectedly.

Now the hard part: picking the puppy that will be with you for a good part of your life. Narrow your choice to the ones that fit your previous decisions regarding sex, color, coat type, and size. A rule of thumb is that adult Chihuahuas will weigh roughly twice as much as they do when they are 12 weeks old.

In general, by eight weeks of age, Chihuahuas look like Chihuahuas, only even smaller. Heads should be comparatively large and rounded, with a right angle between the forehead and muzzle. Ears may or may not be standing at this age; even if standing, they may flop again during teething periods. If ears are not standing by ten weeks of age, an experienced breeder or veterinarian can show you how to tape the ears to encourage them to stand. Most dogs have erect ears by four or five months of age; don't give up all hope until after six months. Pups should be fairly steady on their feet and not excessively cowhocked or exhibit any abnormal kinks and bends in their limbs.

Eyes, ears, and nose should be free of discharge or debris. A watery discharge from the eyes is not uncommon in Chihuahuas and does not indicate disease, but may continue throughout life and cause tear stains on the fur. The teeth should be straight and meet up evenly, with the top incisors just overlapping the lower incisors. Crooked teeth and undershot bites will only get worse with age.

The puppies should be clean, with no missing hair, crusted or reddened skin, nor signs of parasites. The gums should be pink; pale gums may indicate anemia. The area around the anus should have no hint of irritation or recent diarrhea. Puppies should not be thin or excessively potbellied. The belly should have no large bumps indicating a hernia. By the age of eight weeks, male puppies should have both testicles descended in the scrotum; if not present by 12 weeks, there is little hope.

Normal Chihuahua puppies are friendly, curious, and attentive. Shy away from a shy puppy. You are usually safest to pick the average pup from a litter, neither the boldest nor quietest. If pups are apathetic or sleeping, it could be because they have just eaten, but it could also be because they are sickly. If the puppy of your choice is limping, or exhibits any of the above traits, express your concern and ask to either come back next week to see if it has improved, or to have your veterinarian examine it.

In fact, any puppy you buy should be done so with the stipulation that the sale is pending a health check of the pup (at your expense) by your veterinarian. The breeder should furnish a complete medical history including dates of vaccinations and worming.

As you study these canine Mexican jumping beans, you may suddenly find it impossible to be objective. How will you ever decide which one to take home? If you want a show puppy, let the breeder decide. In fact, the breeder knows the puppies' personalities better than you will in the short time you can evaluate them, so listen carefully to any suggestions the breeder has even for a pet.

If you can't decide which bouncing baby will be yours, don't worry: no matter which one you choose, it will be the best one. In years to come, you will wonder how you were so lucky to have picked the most loving Chihuahua in the world, but you must realize that your Chihuahua will be wonderful in part because you are going to make it that way!

The Chihuahua Checklist

Is your home really ready to accommodate a new bouncing baby Chihuahua? Don't wait until you have a puppy underfoot before you realize major changes need to be made. Your pup will keep you busy enough with routine matters, and besides, you'll want to spend those first days playing and snuggling, not home redecorating.

Chihuahuas, Chew Toys, and Checkbooks

One of the best things about having a new puppy is that you now have a reason to go on a major, uninhibited shopping spree for all sorts of Chihuahua essentials. A visit to a large pet store, a dog show vendor aisle, or a glance through one of the many pet supply mail-order catalogs will regale you with items you never imagined a dog could need. But even if shopping is not your idea of fun, there are a few essentials you must have.

Chihuahuas love toys. A ball, of course, is a necessity, but be sure it is not small enough to be inhaled. Many Chihuahuas will take very good care of stuffed animal toys. Latex squeaky toys are also enjoyable (for them, but not always to their owners!); make sure the squeaker is secure. Homemade toys of stuffed socks are also big favorites.

Dogs, and especially teething puppies, chew. Teething human babies are given teething rings, but teething canine babies are too often only given a firm correction. Instead, they should be given rawhide or nylon bones to satisfy the urge.

Chihuahuas are definitely "toy" dogs. Two kinds of toys popular with Chihuahuas are soft stuffed animals and latex squeaky toys.

Of course, your Chihuahua will want to be well dressed. In cold climates, Chihuahuas appreciate wearing a doggy sweater or coat. In any climate, your Chihuahua will need a collar or harness. A harness has the advantage of applying pressure to the dog's chest, rather than its neck. A collar is easier to take on and off, and is more comfortable for wearing around the house; try a cat safety collar. Chihuahuas have such sensitive skin that wearing either a collar or harness continually can result in hair loss and skin irritation. If a collar is worn outside of the home, take care that it cannot possibly slip over the dog's head. A lightweight leash is another necessity (a show lead or cat leash works well). Never use a chain leash with a Chihuahua.

You will need flat-bottomed food and water bowls, preferably stainless steel. Some dogs can have an allergic reaction to plastic, and cracks in ceramic can hold bacteria. Be sure to find out what your puppy is eating and try to feed the same food. Although your young Chihuahua won't require

Rawhide chewies are a necessity for many Chihuahuas, especially teething puppies.

Two lucky Chihuahuas enjoy a comfortable bed, the next best thing to Mom's or Dad's lap.

much grooming, you will still need a soft brush and some nail clippers. You should also assemble your first aid kit.

Chihuahua Quarters

No doubt you have your own bed where you sleep at night. Where will your puppy's bed be? Even if you eventually plan to share your bed with your Chihuahua, it's best not to start out that way. For one thing, your bed is too high for the puppy to get on and off of at will, and it could easily hurt itself trying to do so. For another, you could crush a tiny puppy. Finally, it is best not to accustom the puppy to always being in your bed, because there will likely be times when that is not possible.

Your Chihuahua will appreciate having its own private bed readily available whenever sleep overtakes it. Puppies will chew wicker, so save the traditional wicker basket for a later age. For a baby, any small box will do, as long as it is abundantly lined with soft blankets.

A crate or cage is an ideal bed, an invaluable house-training tool, and a means of keeping your puppy out of trouble when you can't always watch. Think of it as you would a baby's crib: a place for peace and protection. And just as with a child, the crib or crate is a place for bedtime and naptime, but not a place of exile or a place to spend entire days. Plastic crates are readily available and economical. Wire crates allow more ventilation and visibility.

Baby gates are also a big help; puppies do not protest as much when blocked by a baby gate as when blocked by a closed door, plus you can keep an eye on them. Some of the anti-chew preparations may help protect your furniture and walls, but do not rely exclusively upon them. Toys, chew bones, and a keen eye are the best furniture protectors.

Although Chihuahuas enjoy sunning themselves outdoors on nice days, they are decidedly not outdoor dogs and should only be acquired with the idea that they will live in the house. One of the many advantages to raising a small dog is that you can set up a tiny yard for it right in your living room. A child's playpen can be a handy place to put the pup when you can't watch it constantly. Larger wire pens can be bought (so called exercise pens, or "X-pens") at dog shows or better pet stores, or you can make one out of PVC pipe. If the pen is large enough, the dog's bed or crate can be placed in one corner, some newspaper in the other, its food and water in another, and its toys everywhere. This setup is ideal if you work or must leave the puppy for extended periods of time.

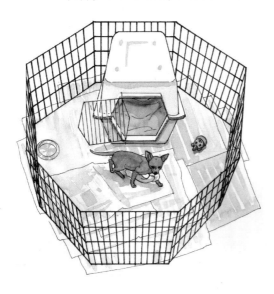

An X-pen provides a secure compound for a Chihuahua when it must be left alone.

New puppies should never have the run of the entire house. Choose an easily Chihuahua-proofed room where you spend a lot of time, preferably one that is close to a door leading outside. Kitchens and dens are usually ideal. When you must leave your dog for some time, you may wish to place it in its crate or X-pen. Bathrooms have the disadvantage of being so confining and isolated that puppies may become destructive; garages have the disadvantage of also housing many poisonous items.

If you live in a warm climate where you can keep your Chihuahua outside while you are gone, you must provide shelter, preferably a cozy doghouse. Some people combine a kennel run with a doggy door leading to an enclosure in a garage, or to a separate room in the house.

Safeguarding Your Chihuahua

The first step in Chihuahua-proofing your home is to do everything you would do to baby-proof your home— and more! Put poisons out of reach; rodent baits, household cleaners, leaked antifreeze, drugs, some house-plants, and even chocolate (especially baker's chocolate) can be deadly, especially for a small dog. Antifreeze is an especially insidious killer: it has a sweet taste that dogs adore, and a toxic effect that will kill unless treated immediately. Pennies, needles, nails, bones, rocks, and rings have all been found in puppies' stomachs, and all have proved fatal at times.

Get down at puppy level and see what dangers beckon. Puppies love to chew electrical cords, and even lick outlets. These can result in severe burns, loss of the jaw or tongue, or death. Running into a sharp furniture corner could cause an eye or head injury. A Chihuahua with an open fontanel must be guarded against hitting the top of its head on the edges or bottom of furniture, and should ideally not be allowed under furniture at all. Jumping up could cause an unstable object to come crashing down, perhaps crushing the puppy. Do not allow the puppy near the edges of high decks, balconies, or staircases.

If you plan to allow your puppy up on furniture, you will have to make sure it has a way to get back off without getting hurt. Too many owners fall asleep on the sofa with the pup in their arms, only to awake to a crying injured dog that has fallen or jumped off. Chihuahuas tend to have a relatively heavy body in comparison to their petite bone size, and this can place extra stress on bones and joints when jumping. A makeshift ramp or steps is a good idea for Chihuahuas of any age if they are to be furniture dogs.

Doors can be a hidden danger area. Everyone in your family must be made to understand the danger of slamming a door, which could catch a Chihuahua and break a leg—or worse. Use doorstops to ensure that the wind does not blow doors suddenly shut, or that the puppy does not go behind the door to play. This can be a danger, because the gap on the hinged side of the door can catch and break a little Chihuahua leg if the door is closed. Be especially cautious with swinging doors; a puppy may try to push one open, become caught, try to back out, and strangle. Clear glass doors may not be seen, and the puppy could be injured running into them. Garage doors and dogs can be a deadly combination. Finally, doors leading to unfenced outdoor areas should be kept securely shut.

Now do the same search in your yard. Are there bushes with sharp, broken branches at Chihuahua eye level? Are there trees with dead branches in danger of falling, or even heavy falling fruits or pinecones? Both of the latter have killed unlucky Chihuahuas. Are there poisonous

Get down at puppy level to see what dangers await your Chihuahua.

plants? Some of the more deadly are yew, mistletoe, English holly berries, philodendron, Jerusalem cherry, azaleas, rhododendron, foxglove, water hemlock, milkweed, rattlebox, corn cockle, jimsonweed, jessamine, oleander, and castor bean. If you have a pool, be aware that although dogs are natural swimmers, a little Chihuahua cannot get out of most swimming pools and can eventually drown.

Although it's difficult to guard against them, be on the lookout for biting and stinging insects. Use an insect repellent if your dog must stay outside for long periods. If your dog is stung, remove the stinger and watch to make sure there is no allergic reaction. Fire ants could seriously injure a puppy. And beware the toad: a large toad secretes a poisonous substance that could make a puppy very ill; the giant marine toad can be deadly.

Chihuahuas, like all dogs, would love to run loose and rule the neighborhood. But they probably wouldn't live long if they did. Because

Chihuahuas are blissfully ignorant of the dangers that lurk for a little dog in the big outdoors, it is vital that you prevent such roaming. Luckily, Chihuahuas are not known for their fence jumping prowess, but they are adept burrowers. A small hole in the fence is all one needs to wriggle its way to freedom. Many dogs are actually inadvertently taught to escape by their owners. Perhaps the owners had an old fence when they got their new pup, and figured they'd see if it would hold the dog. When the dog squeezes out of the biggest holes, the owner patches those. Then the dog looks for the next biggest hole, and squeezes out of it. Finally, as the fence comes to resemble a patchwork quilt, the dog is squeezing through holes that you would swear couldn't possibly accommodate a dog with bones. Yet, if the fence only had such tiny holes in the first place, the dog would never have learned to go through them. If you wanted your Chihuahua to learn to squeeze through small passages, wouldn't you do so a little at a time? Then why use the same tactic to teach your dog *not* to squeeze through? If you want your dog to stay in the yard, make the yard Chihuahua-proof from the very beginning.

You must protect your tiny dog against the dangers of other animals. Your fence must not only be strong enough to keep your dog in, but to keep stray dogs out. This is why the "invisible fences" that keep your dog within are no good for Chihuahuas. They don't keep other dogs out. If you live in a rural area, wild animals (including alligators, coyotes, and hawks) may look upon your puppy as a snack.

Safeguarding Your Home

You've protected your Chihuahua, now how about your home? If you have carpeting, consider covering it with small washable rugs or a strip of indoor-outdoor carpeting until your puppy is housebroken, at least in the area between the crate and the door. If you use an X-pen, cover the floor beneath it with thick plastic (an old shower curtain works well), and then add towels or washable rugs for traction and absorbency.

Remove anything breakable that you value from your Chihuahua's reach. Puppies particularly like to chew items that carry your scent. Shoes, socks, eyeglasses, and clothing must be kept out of the youngster's reach. Remove books and papers. Chihuahua pups love confetti!

Life with a Chihuahua

The Homecoming

Spend some time at the breeder's house while the puppy gets acquainted with you, and listen carefully to the breeder's instructions. Arrange for the puppy not to have eaten before leaving with you; this lessens the possibility of car sickness and helps the puppy learn that you will be its new provider when you get to its new home. If you work, try to bring the pup home on a weekend so that the first day in its new home won't be one spent alone. The ride home with you may be the puppy's first time in a car, and its first time away from the security of its home and former family. Be sure to take plenty of towels in case it gets carsick. If possible, bring a family member to hold and comfort the puppy on the ride home. If it is a long ride, bring a cage. Never let a new puppy roam around the car, where it can cause, and have, accidents.

Incidentally, be sure to ask the breeder what name your puppy knows. Most breeders call all of their puppies by some generic name, such as "Pup." Just continue to call yours by the same name until you have something better picked out. Your pup will learn a new name quickly at this age, especially if it means food or fun is on the way. Be careful about the name you choose; for example, "Gnome" starts with a sound that is too similar to "No," and "Kay" sounds too much like "Stay." Test your chosen name to be sure that it does not sound like a reprimand or command.

When you get home, put the puppy on-lead and carry it to the spot you have decided will be the bathroom. Puppies tend to relieve themselves in areas where they can smell that they have used before. This is why it is so critical to never let the pup have an accident indoors, and if it does, to block its access to that area. Once the puppy relieves itself, let it explore a little and then offer it a small meal. Now is not the time for all the neighbors to come visiting. You want your pup to know who its new family members will be, and more people will only add to the youngster's confusion.

Once the puppy has eaten, it will probably have to relieve itself again, so take it back out to the part of the yard you have designated as the bathroom. Remember to praise enthusiastically when the puppy eliminates in the right place. When your Chihuahua begins to act sleepy, place it in its crate so that it knows this is its special bed. A stuffed toy, hot water bottle, or ticking clock may help alleviate some of the anxiety of being left alone. You may wish to place the crate in your bedroom for this first night so that the puppy may be comforted by your presence. Remember, this is the scariest thing that has ever happened in your puppy's short life; it has been uprooted from the security of a mother, littermates, and a loving breeder, so you must be comforting and reassuring on this crucial first night.

Housebreaking

Chihuahuas, like all canines, have a natural desire to avoid soiling their denning area. As soon as young wolves are able to walk, they will teeter out of their den to relieve themselves away from their bedding. Your Chihuahua will do the same. But you want your puppy to do more than just step just outside the door of the crate and eliminate there; you want it to go outside!

Puppies have very weak control over their bowels, so that if you don't take them to their elimination area often, they may not be able to avoid soiling. Forcing a puppy to soil its crate will have a detrimental effect upon housebreaking, and will also give you a distasteful cleanup problem. If the cage is too large for the puppy, it may simply step away from the area it sleeps in and relieve itself at the other end of the crate, which may help the puppy to keep clean but will in no way help housebreak it. An overly large crate can be divided with a secure barrier until the puppy is larger or housebroken.

To avoid accidents, learn to predict when your puppy will have to relieve itself. Immediately after awakening, and soon after heavy drinking or playing, your puppy will urinate. You will probably have to carry a younger puppy outside to get it to the elimination area on time. Right after eating, or if nervous, your puppy will have to defecate. Circling, whining, sniffing, and generally acting worried usually signals that defecation is imminent. Even if the puppy starts to relieve itself, quickly but calmly scoop the pup up and carry it outside (the surprise of being picked up will usually cause the puppy to stop in midstream, so to speak). You can add a firm "No," but yelling and swatting are neither necessary nor effective. When the puppy does relieve itself in its outside bathroom, remember to heap on the praise and let your Chihuahua puppy know how pleased you are.

The more the pup soils in a particular spot, the more it is likely to return to that same spot. So, one of the most important keys to successful housebreaking is to never let the first accident occur. Once it has (and more than likely it will), deodorize the area thoroughly, using a non-ammonia-based cleaner, and if possible, place it on the off-limits list, at least temporarily. There are products on the market that use urine scent to encourage a puppy to urinate on them as a housebreaking aid.

You may wish to paper train your puppy. Place newspapers on the far side of the room (or X-pen), away from the puppy's bed or water bowl; near a door to the outside is best. Place the puppy on the papers as soon as it starts to relieve itself. A convenient aspect of paper training is that the concept of using the paper will transfer to wherever you put the paper, so if you later take the paper outside it can act as a training tool there. You can also litter box train your puppy. Place newspaper or even cat litter in a cat box; add some soiled newspaper or something with the scent of urine, and place the pup in the box when it begins to urinate. Apartment dwellers may find that a box-trained Chihuahua is very convenient on rainy days.

No matter how intellectually gifted your Chihuahua is, it probably will not have full control over its bowels until it is around six months of age. Meanwhile, set the stage for a perfect house pet, and chin up! It will get better!

A Little Dog in a Big World

Most people who live with Chihuahuas are perfectly content to cuddle with them and share adventures around the house, and their Chihuahua, too, will be perfectly content. But even a little Chihuahua can be a lively and versatile partner in a safari in the neighborhood park. But beware that walking a Chihuahua entails many dangers that most dog owners never have to consider. If you are walking around the neighborhood, use a harness or a collar that will not slip over your Chihuahua's head, a 6-foot (1.8 m) lightweight leash, or a longer lightweight retractable leash. Be very careful with retractable leashes; when dropped, the handle retracts quickly toward the dog and some puppies think it is chasing them, causing them to run from it in fright! Also, dogs can still get in plenty of trouble when on these leashes, so don't be lulled into a false sense of security just because the dog is on-lead. Always remember to think little; could your Chihuahua fall into that rain gutter?

As a Chihuahua walker, you must take precautions in order to protect your little dog from loose dogs that may attack. Never let your Chihuahua off-lead where there are other dogs off-lead. They could mistake the tiny Chihuahua for a prey animal or simply attack it as they might any dog; as tough as Chihuahuas may think they are, such attacks can prove deadly. Do not walk your Chihuahua by yourself if you cannot fend off stray dogs. Carrying a basket in which to hide your Chihuahua if trouble begins is a good idea, and even carrying a dog-repellent spray for the worst case scenario is wise. Your Chihuahua may protect you from bad people, but you must protect it from bad dogs.

Pick a regular time of day to walk and try to stick to it. Your Chihuahua will come to expect a walk at this time and won't fall for any of your excuses. Keep up a good pace, but don't expect your Chihuahua to be your long-distance jogging companion. Be considerate of those little legs pumping as fast as they can go! Check the footpads regularly for signs of abrasion. Hot pavement can blister a dog's feet. Finally, leave your dog at home in hot weather. Dogs are unable to cool themselves through sweating, and heatstroke in jogging dogs is a common emergency seen by veterinarians in the summer. Chihuahuas are more susceptible to heat stress than are many other breeds.

Besides watching for loose dogs, there are many other dangers that lurk for the free-running Chihuahua. Never allow your friend to run loose in sight of traffic. Although your dog may usually stay with you, keep in mind that a cat, children, or an enticing scent can lure your dog away and cause it to end up in potentially dangerous places. Unfortunately, there are very few places that a Chihuahua can be let loose safely. A fenced ball field or tennis court may be a possibility, as long as you clean up after your dog vigilantly.

As a youngster, your puppy is the best judge of how much exercise is best. Do not encourage jumping either up or down. Never force a youngster to go beyond its limits. By the time your puppy becomes an adult, you can begin to work up to longer play periods or walking distances. Regular exercise is absolutely essential to good physical and mental health of your dog. Although Chihuahuas can get a workout running from one end of the house to the other, they will appreciate the mental workout and variety afforded by a walk outdoors.

On the Road with Your Chihuahua

Its small size, protective demeanor, and desire to be by its owner's side makes a Chihuahua a natural traveling companion. You may find that sharing a trip with your Chihuahua, especially if you would otherwise be traveling alone, can be a rewarding experience. But do consider that traveling with any dog sets limits on where you can go. Many motels do not accept even small

Short car trips with ample time for the chihuahua to play outside helps to train a puppy to overcome carsickness.

pets, and many attractions have no facilities for temporary pet boarding. Most beaches, and many state parks, do not allow dogs. There are several publications listing motels that do accept dogs (e.g., *Touring with Towser*) and many major attractions have dog boarding facilities on their grounds, but some are not adequate for a Chihuahua.

Sometimes the rules against dogs seem so very unfair. Unfortunately, in many cases they are the only self-defense that establishments have against irresponsible dog owners. Even a little Chihuahua can do its share of damage. Barking in motel rooms, urinating on motel rugs, defecating in walking areas, and snapping at friendly passersby can create problems for everyone. The next time you are turned away from a motel with your dog, you can thank those owners who think their adorable dogs are immune from the rules. Please do not be one of them.

Ideally your Chihuahua should always ride with the equivalent of a doggy seat belt: the cage. Many dogs have emerged from their cages shaken but safe, from accidents that would have otherwise proved fatal. A cage can also help prevent accidents if you have a Chihuahua that thinks it should be driving. The least safe place for your Chihuahua to ride is in the driver's lap. Never let your Chihuahua hang out of the window while you are driving; not only can it get foreign bodies in its eyes, but it could also fall out. And always be careful that your Chihuahua doesn't jump out of the car when you stop.

Nothing can spoil a road trip like a carsick dog. Car sickness is a common ailment of puppies; most outgrow it, but some need car training in order to overcome it. Initial car rides should be made extremely short, with the object being to complete the ride before the dog gets sick. Driving to a

An X-pen can provide a portable and safe yard-away-from-home when on the road.

place where the dog can get out and enjoy itself before returning home also seems to help the dog look forward to car rides and overcome car sickness. Obviously your dog shouldn't have a full stomach, but sometimes just a little food on its stomach may help. Motion sickness medication may be prescribed by your veterinarian to help in stubborn cases.

Traveling in summer can be difficult. Even on relatively cool days, the temperature in a closed car can rise rapidly to fatally high levels. But Chihuahuas are so small that they can slip out of an opened window unless it is barely left open at all. Never tie a dog inside a car because the animal could hang itself. The best solution if you must travel in summer with your Chihuahua is to use a cage with a padlocked door (and padlocked to your car) so that you can leave the windows down.

If your Chihuahua is more of the jet-setter type, you may be able to carry your friend with you in the passenger compartment. Check with the airline way ahead of time to find out what dimensions of a cage can fit beneath the seat, which is where your Chihuahua would ride. Make reservations because usually there is a limit on the number of dogs allowed to ride with the passengers.

Whether you will be spending your nights at a motel, a campground, or even a friend's home, always have your dog on its very best behavior. Ask beforehand if it will be okay for you to bring your Chihuahua. Have your dog clean and parasite-free. Do not allow your Chihuahua pal to run loose at motels or campgrounds, and do not allow it to run helter-skelter through the homes of friends. Bring your dog's own clean blanket or bed, or better yet, its crate. Your dog will appreciate the familiar place to sleep, and it will keep your Chihuahua out of danger. After all, you can't expect your

When Traveling with Your Pet

The suitcase for the well-prepared Chihuahua traveler should include:

- A first aid kit.
- Heartworm preventive.
- Any other medications.
- Food and water bowls.
- Dog biscuits and chewies.
- Flea spray.
- A flea comb.
- A brush.
- A change of bedding.
- Short and long leashes.
- A sweater.
- A flashlight.
- Plastic baggies or other poop disposal means.
- Moist towelettes.
- Paper towels.
- Food.
- The health and rabies certificate.

Besides the regular tags, your dog should wear identification indicating where you could be reached while on your trip, or including the address of someone you know will be at home. Bring a recent color photo in case your Chihuahua somehow gets lost. If you are traveling by car a jug of water from home can be a big help, as many dogs are very sensitive to changes in water and can develop diarrhea.

host to have Chihuahua-proofed his or her home like you have. Even though your dog may be used to sleeping on furniture at home, a proper guest stays on the floor or on its own bedding when visiting. Walk your dog often (and clean up after it) to make sure no accidents occur inside. Never leave your dog unattended in a strange place. The dog's perception is that you have left and forgotten it; it either barks or tries to dig its way out through the doors in an effort to find

you, or becomes upset and relieves itself on the carpet. Make sure your Chihuahua is so well behaved, your host invites both of you back.

Traveling with your Chihuahua will take more work and planning, but you may find that the trip is much more enjoyable because of the presence of your most loyal travel companion.

Boarding

Sometimes you have no choice but to leave your Chihuahua behind when you travel, and may need to board your dog at a kennel or your veterinarian's. Ask friends for recommendations. The ideal kennel will have climate-controlled accommodations, and keep your Chihuahua either indoors or in a combination indoor-outdoor run. Make an unannounced visit to the kennel and ask to see the facilities. Although you can't expect spotlessness and a perfumed atmosphere, most runs should be clean and the odor should not be overpowering. All dogs should have clean water and at least some dogs (including any Chihuahuas) should have bedding. Good kennels will require proof of immunizations, and an incoming check for fleas. They will allow you to bring toys and bedding, and will administer medication. Strange dogs should not be allowed to mingle, and the entire kennel area should be fenced.

Your dog may be more comfortable if a pet sitter comes to your home and feeds and exercises your dog regularly. This works best if you have a doggy door. Whatever means you choose, always leave emergency numbers and your veterinarian's name.

Little Dog Lost

The most common mistake people make when their dog is missing is to wait in hopes that it will come back. By the time they realize that something is amiss, it is often too late.

34

Better to have a false alarm than a lifetime of regret. If your dog has recently escaped, immediately go to the very worst place you could imagine it going. If you live near a highway, go there, and search backward toward your home. If you still can't find your Chihuahua, get pictures and go door to door; ask any workers or delivery persons in the area. Call the local animal control, police department, and veterinarians. If your dog is tattooed, contact the tattoo registry. Make up *large* posters with a clear picture of your dog. Take out an ad in the local paper. Mention a reward, but do not specify an amount.

Lost dog ads unfortunately set you up as a target for con artists. Never give anyone money before seeing your dog. There are a number of scams involving answering lost dog ads, many asking for money for shipping the dog back to you from a distance or for paying veterinarian bills—when very often these people have not really found your dog. If your dog is tattooed, you can have the person read the tattoo to you in order to positively identify your pet. Other scammers actually steal your dog for reward money, and wait until you are desperate and will pay a high reward; and then have been known to also burglarize your home when you go to meet their partner to pick up the dog! The moral: protect your dog in the first place from theft or loss, and be wary when asked for money in return for your dog.

Your Chihuahua should have a license tag and name tag affixed to its collar, but because it may not always be wearing its collar, it is better to have your dog tattooed. Your Social Security number or your dog's registration number, tattooed on the inside of its thigh, is a permanent and traceable means of identification. You may wish to discuss this option with your veterinarian. Another option is a microchip implant, which is injected under the skin and can hold large quantities of information. The drawback is that a special scanner is needed to read the information, and not all animal shelters can afford these scanners.

Whether or not your dog has a tattoo or microchip implant, it should have a name tag affixed to its collar to provide ready access to some kind of identifying information.

Chihuahua Training the Right Way

What Every Good Chihuahua Trainer Should Know

First of all, nothing will ever go just as perfectly as it seems to in all of the training instructions. But although there may be setbacks, you can train your dog. First, though, you must train yourself. You must be consistent, firm, gentle, realistic, and most of all, patient.

Although no two Chihuahuas are alike, there are some rules that every good Chihuahua trainer should follow:

Name first: The first ingredient in any command is your dog's name. You probably spend a good deal of your day talking, with very few words intended as commands for your dog. So warn your dog that this talk is directed toward it.

Then command: Many trainers make the mistake of simultaneously saying the command word *at the same time* that they are placing the dog into position. *This is incorrect.* The command comes immediately *before* the desired action or position. The crux of training is anticipation: the dog comes to anticipate that after hearing a command, it will be induced to perform some action, and it will eventually perform this action without further assistance from you. On the other hand, when the command and action come at the same time, not only does the dog tend to pay more attention to your action of placing it in position, and less attention to the command word, but the command word loses its predictive value for the dog.

Name, command, action!

Once is enough: Repeating a word over and over, or shouting it louder and louder, never helped anyone, dog or human, understand what is expected. Your Chihuahua is not hard of hearing.

Say what you mean and mean what you say: Your dog takes its commands literally. If you have taught that "Down" means to lie down, then what must the dog think when you yell "Down" to make it stop jumping up on you when you return home? If "Stay" means not to move until given a release word, and you say "Stay here" as you leave the house for work, do you really want your dog to sit by the door all day until you get home?

Think like a dog: In many ways, dogs are like young children; they act to gratify themselves, and they often do so without thinking ahead to consequences. But unlike young children, dogs cannot understand human language (except for those words you teach them), so you cannot explain to them that their actions of five minutes earlier were bad. Dogs live in the present; if you punish them, they can only assume it is for their behavior at the time of punishment. So if you discover a mess, drag your dog to it from its nap in the other room, and scold, the impression to the dog will be that either it is being scolded for napping, or that its owner is mentally unstable. Remember, timing is everything in a correction. If you discover your dog in the process of having an "accident," and snatch the dog up and deposit it

Chihuahuas are adept obedience pupils, but require special handling.

outside, and then yell "No," your dog can only conclude that you have yelled "No" to it for eliminating outside. Correct timing would be "No," quickly take the dog outside, and then praise it once it eliminates outside. In this way, you have corrected the dog's undesired behavior and helped the dog understand desired behavior.

Correct and be done with it: Owners sometimes try to make this "a correction the dog will remember" by ignoring the dog for the rest of the day. The dog may indeed remember that its owner ignored it, but it will not remember why. Again, the dog can only relate its present behavior to your actions.

Never rough: Such methods as striking, shaking, choking, and hang-ing have been touted by some (stupid) trainers: Do not try them! They are extremely dangerous, counterproduc-tive, and cruel; they have no place in the training of a beloved family mem-ber. Chihuahuas are a sensitive breed both mentally and physically, and sel-dom require anything but the mildest of corrections. A direct stare with a harsh "No!" should be all that is required in most cases.

Food is forever: There is nothing wrong with using food as a reward *as long as you intend to continue using it throughout the dog's life*. If you train a dog using food to tell it that it has done well, and then quit rewarding it with food, the impression to the dog is that it has no longer done well. It may eventually quit performing altogether under these circumstances. If you do use food, precede it with praise; that is, praise, then give a tidbit. Also, don't reward with food every time; keep the dog wondering if this will be the time with the tidbit payoff (the slot machine philosophy of dog training). That way, when you can't reward with a tidbit, your Chihuahua will not be surprised and will continue to perform in the absence of food for comparatively long periods. Of course, the advantage of using praise rather than food is that you never can be caught without praise available.

Too much of a good thing: There is such a thing as overpraising a dog throughout the day. Think of it this way: if you spend the day praising and petting your Chihuahua just for breathing, why should it work for your praise later when it can get it for free? Certainly you should praise, pet, and love your Chihuahua, but in some cases of disobedience such "handouts" must be curtailed. Such overindulged Chihuahuas must learn the value of praise by earning it.

Be consistent: Sometimes the puppy can be awfully cute when it misbehaves, or sometimes your hands are full, and sometimes you just aren't sure what you want from your Chihuahua. But lapses in consistency are ultimately unfair to the dog. If you let the pup out of its crate because it whines "just this one time," you have taught the pup that although whining may not always result in freedom, you never know, it just might pay off tonight. In other words, YOU have taught the pup to whine.

Train before meals: Your puppy will work better if its stomach is not full, and will be more responsive to treats if you use them as rewards. Never try to train a sleepy, tired, or hot Chihuahua.

Happy endings: Begin and end each training session with something the dog can do well. And keep sessions short and fun—no longer than 10 to 15 minutes. Dogs have short attention spans and you will notice that after about 15 minutes their performance will begin to suffer unless a lot of play is involved. To continue to train a tired or bored dog will result in the training of bad habits, resentment in the dog, and frustration for the trainer. Especially when training a young puppy, or when you only have one or two different exercises to practice, quit while you are ahead! Keep your Chihuahua wanting more, and you will have a happy, willing, obedience partner.

Dress for Success

Besides the back scratcher and solid leash, equipment for training should include both 6-foot (1.8 m) and 15-foot (4.6 m) lightweight leads. For puppies (as well as shy or easily trained dogs), it is convenient to use

Above is the correct placement of a choke collar. Note: The collar in this illustration is exaggerated in size for clarity. A properly fitted collar should have only about two inches of slack.

one of the lightweight adjustable size show leads. A tough adult can be out-fitted with a small link chain choke collar. The latter has a truly unfortunate name, as it should never be used to choke your Chihuahua. The proper way to administer a correction with a choke collar is with a gentle snap, then immediate release. If you think of the point of the correction as being to startle the dog by the sound of the chain links moving, rather than to choke your dog, you will be correcting with the right level of force, and won't risk jerking your Chihuahua off its feet. The choke collar is placed on the dog so that the ring with the lead attached comes up around the left side of the dog's neck, and through the other ring. If put on backward, it will not release itself after being tightened (because you will be on the right side of your dog for most training). The choke collar should *never* be left on your Chihuahua after a training session; there are too many tragic cases where a choke collar really did earn its name after being snagged on a fence, bush, or even a playmate's tooth.

What Every Good Chihuahua Should Know

Sit: Because Chihuahuas spend so much of their lives looking up, most of them virtually teach themselves to sit as a means of being more comfortable. But you can hasten the process by holding a tidbit above your puppy's eye level, commanding your pet to "Sit," and then moving the tidbit toward your pup until it is slightly behind and above its eyes. When the puppy begins to look up and bend its hind legs, praise, then offer the tidbit. Repeat this, requiring the dog to bend its legs more and more until it must be sitting before receiving praise. This is a much more pleasant way for your puppy to learn its first lesson than the traditional push-pull method of teaching.

For those Chihuahuas that are not natural sitters, or if you do not wish to use a food reward, you will have to help the dog sit. It's easiest if you place "Dixie" on a table where you can easily reach her (but take care that she cannot jump off and hurt herself). After commanding "Dixie, Sit!" push the dog backward slightly with your right hand under her chin, and simul-taneously push forward, gently, behind her "knees," causing them to buckle and the dog to sit. You are, in essence, folding your Chihuahua into a sit.

Stay: Next comes the "stay" com-mand. Tell your puppy to "Sit," praise her, then say "Stay" in a soothing voice (you do not have to precede the "stay" command with the dog's name, because you should already have the dog's attention on you). You should be in the same position that you always have been when teaching the "sit," either beside or directly in front of the dog, or with the dog on the table. If your Chihuahua attempts to get up or lie down, gently place it back into

To teach a Chihuahua to sit, use your right hand to push the dog backward slightly under the chin and your left hand to simul-taneously push it forward behind the knees.

The best time to teach your Chihuahua to come is when it is still a puppy.

position. After only a few seconds, give a release word ("OK!") and praise lavishly. After the dog is staying reliably, change your position relative to it. If you have been beside your dog, step out (starting with your right foot) and turn to stand directly in front of it. Again tell the dog to stay, and gently prevent it from moving. Work up to longer times, and then back away and repeat the process. If you have been training on a table, you need to make the transition to the floor before backing away from the dog. Eventually you should be able to walk confidently away to longer and longer distances, and for longer and longer times. The point is not to push your dog to the limit, but to let it succeed. To do this you must be very patient, and you must increase your times and distances in very small increments. Keep in mind that young puppies cannot be expected to sit for more than 30 seconds at most. When the dog does

move out of position, return and calmly place it back, repeating "Stay"; then return to your position, then return to the dog while it is still staying so that you can praise. Many trainers make the mistake of staring intently at their dog during the "stay," but this is perceived by the dog as a threat and often intimidates them so that they squirm out of position.

Come: When both "Sit" and "Stay" are mastered, you are ready to introduce "Come." Your puppy probably already knows how to come; after all, it comes when it sees you with the food bowl, or perhaps with the leash or ball. You may have even used the word "Come" to get its attention then; if so, you have a head start. You want your puppy to respond to "Dixie, Come" with the same enthusiasm as though you were setting down her supper; in other words, "Come" should always be associated with good things.

Eagerly awaiting its next instruction, this properly trained Chihuahua is both obedient and happy.

Never have your dog come to you and then scold it for something it has done. In the dog's mind, it is being scolded for coming, not for any earlier misdeed.

Make your Chihuahua really want to come running to you by kneeling and calling it enthusiastically.

To teach the command "Come," have your Chihuahua sit, and with the leash attached, command "Stay" and step out to the end of the leash and face your dog. This stay will be a little different for your puppy, as you will drop to your knees, open your arms, and invite her with an enthusiastic "Dixie, Come!" This is obviously not an exercise for tabletop training. An unsure pup can be coaxed with a tug on the lead or the sight of a tidbit. Remember to really praise; after all, you have enticed her to break the "stay" command, and she may be uneasy about that. During the training for "Come," it is not unusual for there to be some regression in the performance of "Stay" due to confusion; just be gentle, patient, and consistent and this will sort itself out.

The next step is to again place the pup in the "sit/stay," walk to the end of the lead, call "Dixie, Come," and quickly back away several steps,

HOW-TO:
Secrets of
Chihuahua Training

Most training classes, training books, and training techniques are geared toward the large, boisterous dog. If you tried some of their corrections on your little Chihuahua, your dog would go sailing across the room!

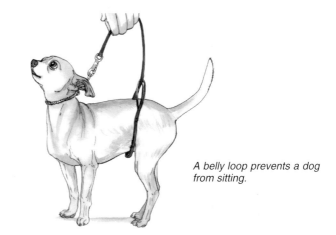

A belly loop prevents a dog from sitting.

Training your Chihuahua on a tabletop will help save your back, but at first your pet may be uneasy.

A big problem when training a little dog is how to guide and correct it. If you bend down to position your Chihuahua every time you want it to sit, you will probably have a bad back before you have a sitting dog. Try some of these small dog solutions:

• Teach stationary exercises on a tabletop or other raised surface. This allows you to have eye contact with your dog and gives you a better vantage from which to help your dog learn.
• To train your dog at your feet,

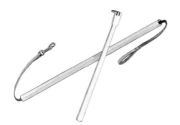

A back scratcher and solid leash are essential training aids for Chihuahuas.

extend your arm length with a back scratcher, with which you can guide and even pet your dog without having to bend over.
• A leash that comes from several feet overhead has virtually no guiding ability whatsoever. You need a lower pivot point for the leash in relation to the dog, and you can achieve this by what is called a "solid leash." This is simply a hollow, light tube, such as PVC pipe, about 3 feet (0.9 m) long, through which you string your leash.
• To prevent a small dog from sitting or lying down, loop part of your regular leash around its belly and hold onto that part, so you have a convenient "handle."

coaxing the dog to you. Eventually you can go to a longer line, and walk quickly backward as far as your equilibrium will allow. This encourages the pup to come at a brisk pace; in fact most dogs will regard this as an especially fun game! Of course, in real life the dog is seldom sitting when you want it to come, so once it understands what you mean by come, allow the pup to walk on-lead, and at irregular intervals call "Dixie, Come," run backward, and when she reaches you, be sure to praise. Finally, attach a longer line to the pup, allow her to meander about, and in the midst of her investigations, call, walk backward, and praise.

You can teach the "down" command by luring the dog toward the floor with a tidbit.

"Come" is the most important command your dog will ever learn. As your dog gets older you will want to practice this command in the presence of distractions, such as other leashed dogs, unfamiliar people, cats, and cars. Always practice on-lead. If it takes a tidbit as a reward to get your Chihuahua motivated, then this is an instance where you should use an occasional food reward. Coming on command is more than a cute trick; it could save your Chihuahua's life.

Down: When you need your Chihuahua to stay in one place for any long periods of time, it is best for it to be left in a "down/stay." Begin teaching the "down" command with the dog in the sitting position. If you are using food rewards, command "Dixie, Down," then show her a tidbit and move it below her nose toward the ground. If she reaches down to get it, give it to her. Repeat, requiring her to reach farther down (without lifting her rear from the ground) until she has to lower her elbows to the ground. You can help her out here by reaching over her and easing her front legs out in front of her.

If you do not wish to use food rewards, again start with the dog sitting, command "Dixie, Down," then place your left hand over her shoulders and with your right hand gently grasp both front legs and ease her to the ground. Never try to cram your dog into the down position, which could not only cause injuries, but scare a submissive dog and cause a dominant dog to resist.

Practice the "down/stay" just as you did the "sit/stay." In fact, your dog now has quite a repertoire of behaviors that you can combine in different ways to combat boredom. The only thing left for any well-behaved Chihuahua is the ability to walk politely on-lead.

Heel: Although in many public situations it is safer to carry your Chihuahua, your dog should still know how to walk nicely on a leash. An untrained Chihuahua on a leash can actually be more dangerous to its owner than many large dogs are to theirs because a Chihuahua can dart underfoot and cause its owner to trip. It is also a danger to itself, because it can be stepped on if it gets out of position. So more than most breeds, it is essential that a Chihuahua be trained to the heel position.

Proper heel position will keep your dog safely beside you.

The first step is to introduce your puppy to the leash, using the lightweight show-type lead. If you have followed this training sequence, your pup should already be acquainted with the leash at least by the time it has learned "Come." Still, walking alongside of you on-lead is a new experience for a young puppy, and many will freeze in their tracks once they discover their freedom is being violated. In this case, do not simply drag the pup along, but coax it with praise, and if need be, food, until it's walking somewhere—anywhere. When the puppy follows you, praise and reward. In this way, the pup comes to realize that following you while walking on-lead pays off.

Once your Chihuahua walks confidently on-lead, it is time to ask for more. Using the solid leash, have your Chihuahua sit in the heel position; that is, on your left side with its neck next to and parallel with your leg. Say "Dixie, Heel" and step off with your left foot first (remember that you stepped off on your right foot when you left your dog on a "stay"; if you are consistent, the foot that moves first will provide an eye-level cue for your little dog). During your first few practice sessions, you will keep her on a short lead, holding her in the heel position, and of course praising her. When you stop, have her sit. Although some trainers advocate letting the dog lunge to the end of the lead and then snapping it back, such an approach is unfair if you haven't shown the dog what is expected of it at first, and such methods are not appropriate for a Chihuahua. Nor is the suggestion of allowing the dog to get in front of you and then stepping on it. That's not safe for either of you! Instead, after a few sessions of showing the dog the heel position, give her a little more loose lead; if she stays in the heel position, praise; more likely she will not, in which case pull her back to position with a quick gentle snap, then release, of the lead. If, after a few days of practice, your dog still seems oblivious to your efforts, turn unexpectedly several times; teach your dog that it is its responsibility to keep an eye on you.

Keep up a good pace; too slow a pace gives dogs time to sniff, to look all around, and, in general, become distracted; a brisk pace will focus the dog's attention upon you and generally aid training. As you progress, you will want to add some right, left, and about-turns, and walk at all different speeds. Then practice in different areas (still always on-lead) and around different distractions. Vary your routine to combat boredom, and keep training sessions short. Adult dogs should be taught that heeling is not the time to relieve themselves.

Mind Games

Although sitting and staying and the like are necessary for good manners,

Teach your dog the "sit up" command by holding a tidbit above its head while it is in the "sit" position.

they don't exactly astound your friends. For that you need something flashy, some incredible feat of intelligence and dexterity: a dog trick. Try the standards: roll over, play dead, catch, sit up, jump the stick, speak. All are easy to teach with the help of the same obedience concepts outlined in the training section. You will find that your particular dog is more apt to perform in ways that make some tricks easier than others to teach. Most Chihuahuas are easy to teach to "speak"; wait until it appears your dog will bark, say "speak," and then reward with a treat after the bark. A dog that likes to lie on its back is a natural for "roll over"; give the command when the dog is already on its back, then guide the dog the rest of the way over with a treat. If your dog can physically do it, you can teach it when to do it.

Higher Education

Is your Chihuahua "gifted?" Perhaps you would like to take it to obedience classes, where both of you can learn even more, practice around distractions, and discuss problems with people who have similar interests. Most cities have obedience clubs that conduct classes. The AKC or your local Humane Society can direct you to them. You might also contact one of the Chihuahua breed clubs and ask for names of Chihuahua obedience enthusiasts in your area. Attend a local obedience trial (contact the AKC for date and location) and ask local owners of happy working dogs (especially Chihuahuas!) where they train. Be aware that not all trainers may understand the Chihuahua psyche, and not all classes may be right for you and your Chihuahua.

You may wish to enter an obedience trial yourself eventually, in which case the advice of fellow competitors will be invaluable. Obedience competitors love their sport; they love to welcome newcomers, and they love to see them succeed; most of all they love their dogs and understand how you love yours. Chihuahuas are adept obedience pupils, and you and your dog could very well become a star team.

Obedience Trials

You plan on training your Chihuahua the commands heel, sit, down, come, and stay for use in everyday life. Add the "stand for exam" (also useful in everyday life, for example, at the veterinarian's), and your dog will have the basic skills necessary to earn the AKC Companion Dog (CD) title. The AKC will send you a free pamphlet describing obedience trial regulations. Higher degrees of Companion Dog Excellent (CDX) or Utility Dog (UD) also require retrieving, jumping, hand signals, and scent discrimination. Chihuahuas have to overcome some hardships due to their size at trials, but many have proven that they have what it takes. And in case you think Chihuahuas can't use their noses, several have also earned Tracking Dog (TD) titles, requiring them to follow a trail by scent.

As a Chihuahua owner, you must always exercise more caution than the average dog owner. Let other members of your obedience class know that your dog could be injured by theirs if they do not keep theirs under control. Ask the judge at an obedience trial to move your dog away from large dogs during the group stays. Better safe than sorry!

If you enter competition with your Chihuahua, remember this as your Golden Rule: Companion Dog means just that; being upset at your dog because it messed up defeats the purpose of obedience as a way of promoting a harmonious partnership between trainer and dog. Failing a trial, in the scope of life, is an insignificant event. Never let a ribbon or a few points become more important than a trusting relationship with your companion. Besides, your Chihuahua will forgive you for the times you mess up!

The Canine Good Citizen

In order to formally recognize dogs that behave in public, the AKC offers the Canine Good Citizen (CGC) certificate. To pass this test, your Chihuahua must demonstrate that it will walk quietly with you around other people; sit for examination; not jump up on, act aggressively toward, or shy from someone who greets you; and stay in place without barking. The CGC is perhaps the most important title that your Chihuahua can earn. The most magnificent champion in the show ring is no credit to its breed if it is not a good public citizen in the real world.

Even Chihuahuas Misbehave

Even a pint-size pup can cause a truckload of trouble for itself and others. Although their owners may not like to admit it, Chihuahuas are still dogs and share the behavioral problems to which all dogs are prone. Behavioral problems are the leading reason that dogs are relinquished to animal shelters. Yet many of these problems can be avoided or cured.

Barking

Chihuahuas are definitely a breed where the bark is worse than the bite. But the bark can be pretty bad. Barking is a natural and useful trait of dogs, and having a Chihuahua doorbell is rather handy. But there is a difference between a dog that will warn you of a suspicious stranger and one that will warn you of a falling leaf. Luckily the Chihuahua bark is not overwhelming, but if you live in an apartment or other close quarters, the surest way to make your neighbors dislike your dog is to let it bark excessively. Allow your Chihuahua to bark momentarily at strangers, and then call it to you and praise for quiet behavior. Distract it with an obedience exercise if need be.

Isolated dogs will often bark as a means of getting attention and alleviating loneliness. Even if the attention gained includes punishment, the dog will continue to bark in order to obtain the temporary presence of the owner. The simplest solution is to move the dog's domain to a less isolated location. For example, if barking occurs when your pup is put to bed, move its bed into your bedroom. If this is not possible, the pup's quiet behavior must be rewarded by the owner's presence, working up to gradually longer and longer periods. The distraction of a special chew toy, given only at bedtime, may help alleviate barking. The pup who must spend the day home alone is a greater challenge. Again, the simplest solution is to change the situation, perhaps by adding another animal—a good excuse to get two Chihuahuas!

Digging and Chewing

Many a Chihuahua owner has returned home to a scene of carnage and suspected that some mad dog must have broken in the house and gone berserk; after all, those little Chihuahua teeth and paws could never wreak such havoc. They may be small, but they're determined and quick, and a Chihuahua can do its share of home destruction when left alone.

Adult dogs may dig or destroy items through frustration or boredom. The best way to deal with these dogs is to provide both physical interaction (such as chasing a ball) and mental interaction (such as practicing a few simple obedience commands) on a daily basis.

One of the most common causes of destructive behavior is also one of the most misunderstood: separation anxiety. Some angelic Chihuahuas turn into demolition dogs when left alone. The owners attribute this Jekyll and Hyde behavior to the dog "spiting" them for leaving, or think that their dog only misbehaves then because it

"Who, me?" Even angels sometimes need guidance.

knows it would be caught otherwise. But an observant owner will notice some things that are different about the dog that destroys only when left alone. For one, the dog often appears to be in a highly agitated state when the owner returns. For another, the sites of destruction are often around doors, windows, or fences, suggestive of an attempt to escape. Such dogs are reacting to the anxiety of being left alone; recall that for a social animal this is a highly stressful situation. But the average owner, upon returning home to such ruin, punishes the dog. This in no way alleviates the anxiety of being left alone; it does, however, eventually create anxiety associated with the owner's return home, and this tends to escalate the destructive behavior. Dogs seem to understand "when the house is in shreds and my owner appears, I get punished" but not to understand "when I chew the house it gets messed up, and I will get punished when my owner appears." If they did, punishment would remedy the problem. It does not.

Instead, owners must realize that they are dealing with a fear response: the fear of being alone. The foolhardiness of punishing a dog for being afraid should be obvious. Instead the dog must be conditioned to overcome its fear of separation. This is done by separating the dog for very short periods of time and gradually working to longer periods, taking care to never allow the dog to become anxious during any session. This is complicated when the owner *must* leave the dog for long periods during the conditioning program. In these cases, the part of the house or yard in which the dog

Apprehension is evident by the lowered ears and tail, as well as the lifted paw.

is left for long periods should be different from the part in which the conditioning sessions take place; the latter location should be the location in which the owner wishes to leave the dog after conditioning is completed. In either case, when the owner returns home, no matter what the condition of the house, greet the dog calmly or even ignore it for a few minutes, to emphasize the point that being left was really no big deal. Then have the dog perform a simple trick or obedience exercise so that you have an excuse to praise it. It takes a lot of patience, and often a whole lot of self-control, but it's not fair to you or your dog to let this situation continue.

House Soiling

When a dog soils the house, several questions must be asked. Was the dog ever really completely housebroken? If the answer is no, you must begin housebreaking anew. Sometimes a housebroken dog will be forced to soil the house because of a bout of diarrhea, and afterward will continue to soil in the same area. If this happens, restrict that area from the dog, and revert to basic housebreaking lessons once again (see Housebreaking, page 29). Submissive dogs may urinate upon greeting you; punishment only makes this "submissive urination" worse. Keep greetings calm, don't bend over or otherwise dominate the dog, and usually this can be outgrown. Some dogs defecate or urinate due to the stress of separation anxiety; you must treat the anxiety to cure the symptom. Older dogs may simply not have the bladder control that they had as youngsters; paper training or a doggy door is the best solution for them. Older spayed females may "dribble"; ask your veterinarian about estrogen supplementation, which may help. And even younger dogs may have lost control due to an infection; several small urine spots are a sign that a trip to the veterinarian is needed. Male dogs may "lift their leg" inside of the house as a means of marking it as theirs. Castration will usually solve this problem; otherwise diligent deodorizing and the use of some dog-deterring odorants (available at pet stores) may help.

Fearfulness

A bold breed by nature, nonetheless the Chihuahua is very much a one-family, or even a one-person, dog, and is often wary of strangers. Some Chihuahuas may be overly wary, however, to the point of being shy or fearful. Your Chihuahua should never be pushed into situations that might overwhelm it. A program of gradual desensitization, with the dog exposed to the frightening person or thing and then rewarded for calm behavior, is time consuming but the best way to alleviate the fear. Never force a dog who is afraid of strangers to be petted by somebody it doesn't know; it in no way helps the dog overcome its fear and is a good way for the stranger to get bitten. Strangers should be asked to ignore shy dogs, even when approached by the dog. Dogs seem to fear the attention of a stranger more than they fear the strangers themselves.

Never coddle your dog when it acts afraid, because it reinforces the behavior. It is always useful if your Chihuahua knows a few simple commands; performing these exercises correctly gives you a reason to praise the dog and also increases the dog's sense of security because it knows what is expected of it. Whether it is a fear of strangers, dogs, car rides, thunder, or being left alone, the concept is the same: never hurry, and never push the dog to the point that it is afraid.

Aggression

Those little Chihuahua teeth can still do considerable damage. The best cure for aggression is prevention, and the best prevention is to carefully select your Chihuahua from a responsible breeder. Chihuahua temperament is described as terrier-like, even in the standard, and terriers are known for their feisty attitudes; thus, many people excuse their Chihuahua's bad manners as being typical of the breed. But a feisty attitude does not mean an aggressive attitude. Even if your Chihuahua lives in the seclusion of your home, you are not doing it any favor by letting a tendency to bite go unchecked. It still must go to the veterinarian, and possibly a boarding kennel, and its experience in these situations will be a lot more pleasant if strangers can handle it without fear of being bitten. Add to this the fact that Chihuahuas are often irresistible to young children, who may go to pet your dog before you realize it, and you may have a dog bite on your hands.

One of the charms of the Chihuahua is its protective attitude concerning its territory and master. But your pet must learn not to threaten guests you have welcomed into your home. Teach your Chihuahua to look forward to guests by rewarding proper behavior, such as sitting and staying, in the guests' presence. Have the guest offer the dog a tidbit when it acts in a civil fashion.

Some Chihuahuas may bite out of fear, perhaps because the owner is forcing them to be petted by a stranger. The solution is to find out what the dog is afraid of and treat the fear. Be aware that unlike in humans, where direct eye contact is seen as a sign of sincerity, staring a dog directly in the eye is interpreted by the dog as a threat. It can cause a fearful dog to bite out of what it perceives as self-defense.

Some Chihuahuas will bite out of resentment, perhaps because they are always hustled out of the house when company arrives, or in the presence of a new baby. Again, the solution is to teach your dog to respond to simple commands such as sit and stay, and use them to help the dog be well mannered in the presence of guests or the baby. In drastic cases, attention can be withheld from the dog except in the presence of guests or the baby, so that the dog associates being with them as something that brings itself attention and rewards. Of course, it should hardly be mentioned that no baby or child should be allowed to play roughly with or tease your Chihuahua; one could hardly blame a Chihuahua that growls or bites out of self-defense, but one could blame its owner for letting the situation develop.

Aggression toward strange dogs is not uncommon in Chihuahuas, but most owners are smart enough not to let them be foolhardy enough to try to carry out their threats. More problematic is the case where two dogs that live together do not get along. Dogs may be vying for dominance, and fights will occur until one dog emerges as the clear victor. But even in cases where one dog is dominant, fights may erupt when both are competing for the owner's attention. The dominant dog expects to get that attention before the subordinate, but being a fair-minded owner, you may tend to give attention equally, or to even favor the "underdog." This can be interpreted by the dominant dog as an uprising by the subordinate dog, who is then attacked. This is one case where playing favorites (to the dominant dog) will actually be a favor to the subordinate dog in the long run!

At Wit's End

Chances are you and your Chihuahua will live together blissfully with never a major behavioral problem. But if a problem does arise that you are unable to solve, consult your veterinarian. Some problems have physiological bases that can be treated. Also, your veterinarian may refer you to a specialist in canine behavior problems.

The Chihuahua's World

When you share your life with a Chihuahua, you may live in the same physical world, but you don't experience the same sensory world. Your Chihuahua lives in a land of giants, where so much of interest occurs way up in the air. But even when you get down to Chihuahua eye level, your eyes do not see the same thing as your Chihuahua's eyes do. The human eye sees the world in much finer detail and a greater array of colors, than does the canine eye. Dogs can see colors, but their sense of color is like that of what is commonly referred to as a "color-blind" person. That is, they confuse similar shades of yellow-green, yellow, orange, and red, but can see and discriminate blue, indigo, and violet from all other colors and each other as well as people can.

But even the Chihuahuas' tiny nose makes them a giant when compared to humans in the world of odors. It is as though humans are completely blind when it comes to the world of smell, and there is no way you can imagine the vastness of this sensory world that is so very apparent to your dog. The next time you become impatient when your dog wants to sniff something on a walk, consider it the same as when you stop to admire a sunset, much to your Chihuahua's bewilderment.

Dogs also have a well-developed sense of taste, and have most of the

An invitation to play is hard to ignore!

same taste receptors that people do. Research has shown that they prefer meat (big surprise), and although there are many individual differences, the average dog prefers beef, pork, lamb, chicken, and horse meat, in that order.

Even His Master's Voice may sound different to your dog than to you. Dogs can hear much higher tones than can humans, and so can be irritated by high hums from your TV or from those ultrasonic flea collars. The Chihuahua's prick ears are unencumbered by heavy fur and are ideally suited for detecting and localizing sounds, more so than dogs with other ear configurations.

You know, of course, that dogs can feel pain. But because a dog may not be able to express that it is in pain,

you must be alert to changes in your dog's demeanor. A stiff gait, reluctance to get up, irritability, dilated pupils, whining, or limping are all indications that your dog is in pain. Some dogs are more stoic than others, so you must learn to read your individual dog.

Reading your Chihuahua: You must become part naturalist in order to fully appreciate this formerly wild species you have invited into your home. Even the little Chihuahua is a wolf at heart, and you can see your pet exhibit many of the same behavior patterns as its wild ancestors. For example, what does it mean when your Chihuahua greets you with a wagging tail and lips pulled back? Most people would think the dog was snarling, but when combined with a happy, submissive greeting, this facial expression is actually known as a "submissive grin," and is a well-known behavior of wolves.

What if the dog is lowering its body, wagging its tail, holding its tail down, holding its ears down, urinating, and even rolling over? These are all signs of submissive behavior. Punishing this dog for allegedly snarling would be an injustice.

What if the dog greeted you with lips pulled back, but with a high, rigidly held tail, hackles raised, on its toes, with a stiff-legged gait, a direct stare, forward pricked ears, and perhaps lifting its leg to mark a tree? These are all signs of dominant, threatening behavior. This dog is, indeed, snarling, and you had better leave it alone and get help if it is your dog. Approaching or punishing this dog would likely result in a dog bite.

What if the dog greeted you with lips pulled back, maybe a little growl, a

Chihuahua owners can observe wolflike behaviors, such as the interaction between these two playing Chihuahuas, in their own homes. Note the submissive posture of the dog on the right, in response to the dominant posture of the one on the left.

wagging tail, and its front legs and elbows on the ground and rear in the air? This is the classic "play-bow" position, and is an invitation for a game. Take your friend up on it!

Chihuahua owners need to learn to read their pets' body language. Pictured are the postures for aggression (top left), fear (top right), submission (bottom left), and play (bottom right).

Grooming Your Chihuahua

The Long and the Short of It

Whether long or short coated, your Chihuahua will need a short grooming session once or twice a week in order to keep its coat gleaming. Many dogs and owners look forward to such grooming sessions as a relaxing time of bonding. With a short coat, you can use a natural bristle brush to distribute the oils, a rubber bristle brush to remove dead hair, and a flea comb to remove fleas or fine debris.

With a long coat, you will also want to use a pin brush or a wide-tooth comb. You may discover some matting behind the ears or behind the elbows. Because the Chihuahua does not have a very thick undercoat, matting is seldom a problem, but mats are more likely to occur during shedding season or when the hair is oily or dirty. Try to split a mat with your fingers, starting near the skin and pulling it in half longitudinally. Hold the hair between the mat and your dog's skin to avoid painful pulling.

Coat disasters such as stuck on chewing gum can be remedied by first applying ice, pine tar can be loosened with hair spray, and other tar can be worked out with vegetable oil followed by dishwashing detergent. Cornstarch can brighten and fluff a drab, oily coat. Use a soft toothbrush to work on stains. Avoid eye stains by diligent use of an eye stain preventive. Use mineral oil or an ear cleanser to loosen debris in the ear.

Bathing

Chihuahuas rarely need bathing, but when necessary, it is best accomplished in the sink, especially if you have a spray attachment. Use lukewarm water that would be comfortable for you if it were your bath. Place cotton balls in the dog's ears, and wash its entire body before starting on its head. Then rinse the head first and work toward the rear.

You will get better results with a shampoo made for dogs. Dog skin has a pH of 7.5, whereas human skin has a pH of 5.5; bathing in a shampoo formulated for the pH of human skin can lead to scaling and irritation. Most shampoos will kill fleas even if not especially formulated as a flea shampoo, but none has any residual killing action on fleas. In addition,

When bathing your Chihuahua, be sure to use warm water and to place cotton balls in your pet's ears.

there are a variety of therapeutic shampoos for use with skin problems. Dry scaly skin is treated with moisturizing shampoos, excessive scale and dandruff with antiseborrheic shampoos, damaged skin with antimicrobials, and itchy skin with oatmeal-based antipruritics. Finally, no one should be without one of the shampoos that requires no water or rinsing. These are wonderful for puppies, emergencies, and bathing when time does not permit.

The coat of a long-coated Chihuahua is not supposed to stand away from the body, but to conform to the body lines. A coat that is too puffy can be made to lie flatter by using a cream rinse, by wrapping the dog in a towel for drying, or even by putting a stocking (with leg holes cut in it) around the dog while drying. Blow dryers will tend to make the coat puffier, but are otherwise handy for drying once your dog gets used to them. No matter what method you use, take special care that your Chihuahua does not get chilled.

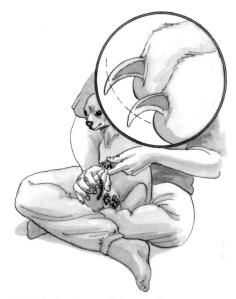

Nail clipping is one of the most important grooming procedures. However, be careful you don't clip too low.

Nail Clipping

When you can hear the pitter-patter of clicking nails, that means that with every step the nails are hitting the floor, and when this happens the bones of the foot are spread, causing discomfort and eventually splayed feet and lameness. If dewclaws are left untrimmed, they can get caught on things more easily or actually loop around and grow into the dog's leg.

Begin by handling the feet and nails daily, and then "tipping" the ends of your puppy's nails every week, taking special care not to cut the "quick" (the central core of blood vessels and nerve endings). Many people find a scissors-type clipper easier to use on

a toy dog than a guillotine nail clipper, but either type is acceptable. You may find it easiest to cut the nails with your Chihuahua lying on its back in your lap, or you may have a helper hold your dog. If you look at the bottoms of the nails, you will see a solid core culminating in a hollowed nail. Cut the tip up to the core, but not beyond. With light-colored nails, you can see the pink inner core of blood vessels, so this is another clue about where to avoid cutting. On occasion, you will slip up and cause the nail to bleed. This is best stopped by styptic powder, but if this is not available, dip the nail in flour or hold it to a wet tea bag. Of course your Chihuahua will use this as an excuse to milk you for all the sympathy you have, but in truth it's not likely to be fatal!

Bathtime should be a pleasant and calm experience.

Wash-and-wear smooth coats still require regular attention in order to keep their coats as sleek and shining as those of these beauties.

Showing off its sparkling coat, this well-groomed long-coated Chihuahua is a sight to behold.

Grooming time should be enjoyable for both owner and dog.

HOW-TO:
Making Fleas Flee

Flea control can be difficult, but with a small dog there is no excuse for fleas to get the upper hand. Any flea control program must be undertaken with care, because overzealous and uninformed efforts may lead to the death of pets as well as fleas. Insecticides can be categorized as organics, natural pesticides, cholinesterase inhibitors, insect growth regulators, and systemics. Incidentally, the ultrasonic flea repelling collars have been shown to be both ineffective on fleas and irritating to dogs. Scientific studies have also shown that feeding dogs brewer's yeast, as has been advocated for years by many dog owners, is ineffective against fleas.

Organics (e.g., D-Limonene) break down the outer shell of the flea and cause death from dehydration. They are safe, but slow acting, and have no residual action. Diatomaceous earth also acts on this same principle;

some researchers have expressed concern that breathing its dust can be dangerous to dogs, however. This is a special concern when dealing with a dog that is as low to the ground as the Chihuahua. Natural grade diatomaceous earth is probably safe; pool grade is probably not.

Natural pesticides (e.g., Pyrethrin, Permethrin, Rotenone) are relatively safe and kill fleas quickly, but have a very short residual action. They do not remain in the dog's system and so can be used frequently.

Cholinesterase inhibitors (e.g., Dursban, Diazinon, Malathion, Sevin, Carbaryl, Pro-Spot, Spotton) act on the nervous systems of fleas, dogs, and humans. They are used in yard sprays, dog sprays and dips, flea collars, and systemics. They kill effectively and have fairly good residual action. But they can poison a dog, especially a tiny dog, if overused, and should never be used on puppies or sick dogs. The systemics are drugs that are applied to the dog's skin for absorption into the blood, or given orally, so that the flea dies when it sucks the blood. It is extremely important

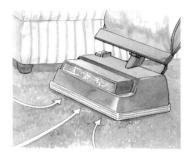

Vacuuming is the first step in the home flea battle. Not only are the fleas vacuumed up, but the vibrations cause fleas to emerge from their pupal state, making them vulnerable to insecticides. Dispose of the vacuum bag afterward.

that you be aware of which chemicals in your arsenal are cholinesterase inhibitors. Using a yard spray in conjunction with systemics, or some sprays and dips, or with certain worm medications that are also cholinesterase inhibitors, can be a deadly combination.

Insect growth regulators (IGRs) prevent immature fleas from maturing and have proven to be the most highly effective method for long-term flea control. Precor is the most widely used for indoor applications, but is quickly broken down by ultraviolet light. Fenoxicarb is better for outdoor use because it is resistant to ultraviolet light. IGRs are nontoxic to mammals but do tend to be expensive. A new type of IGR on the market is the nematode that eats flea larva. Studies show it to be effective and safe, but it must be reapplied regularly because the nematodes die when their food supply (the current crop of flea larva) is gone. Newest on

A wide assortment of flea preparations is available, and owners should be familiar with the properties of each.

the market is lufenuron, a pill given to the dog once a month to sterilize fleas that bite the dog. It is extremely safe, and is available through your veterinarian.

One final warning. There is a popular product on the market that contains "deet" (diethyl-m-toluamide, the same chemical found in some human insect repellents). It has been implicated in the death of many dogs, and is not recommended for Chihuahuas.

If you have only an occasional flea, try using a flea comb, a comb with such finely spaced teeth that it catches fleas between them. Have a cup of alcohol handy for disposing of the fleas. A cotton ball soaked in alcohol and applied

Fleas lay eggs in crevices, as well as in rugs and bedding, so be sure you spray everywhere.

to a flea on the dog will also result in the flea's demise.

Because only about 1 to 10 percent of your home's flea population is actually on your dog, you must concentrate on

treating your home and yard. These are best treated with a combination adult flea killer and IGR. Wash all pet bedding and vacuum other surfaces regularly, and especially before applying insecticides. Be sure that sprays reach into small crevices. Outside, cut grass short and spray in all areas except those that are never shaded (fleas do not mature in these areas). Repeat the entire process 10 to 14 days afterward in order to kill newly emerged fleas.

It may not be easy, but you can win the battle. Every time you feel like giving up, consider how your Chihuahua deserves to live: free of the constant itching caused by a colony of bloodsucking parasites.

In Sickness and in Health

Consult your veterinarian about the proper vaccinations for your Chihuahua.

The Health Check

Because your dog can't talk, and because your veterinarian can't see your dog every day, monitoring your dog's health will be essentially your responsibility. A weekly health check should be part of your grooming procedure. The health check should include examining the eyes for discharge or cloudiness; the ears for bad smell, redness, or discharge; the mouth for red swollen gums, loose teeth, or bad breath; and the skin for parasites, hair loss, or lumps. Observe your dog for signs of lameness or incoordination, or for behavioral change. Weigh your dog and observe whether it is putting on fat or wasting away. Take your Chihuahua to your veterinarian for a yearly checkup, and take geriatric Chihuahuas even more often.

Choosing Your Veterinarian

When choosing your veterinarian, consider availability, emergency arrangements, costs, facilities, and ability to communicate. You and your veterinarian will form a partnership who will work together to protect your Chihuahua's health, so your rapport with your veterinarian is very important. Your veterinarian should listen to your observations, and should explain to you exactly what is happening with your Chihuahua. When you take your Chihuahua to the veterinary clinic, hold your dog on a leash, on your lap, or in a cage; if you think your dog may have a contagious illness, inform the clinic beforehand so that you can use another entrance. Your veterinarian will be appreciative if your Chihuahua is clean and under control during the examination. Warn your veterinarian if you think there is any chance that your dog may bite.

Preventive Medicine

The best preventative medicine is that which prevents accidents: a well-trained dog in a well-fenced yard or on a leash, and a properly Chihuahua-proofed home. Other preventive steps must be taken to avoid diseases and parasites, however.

Vaccinations

Rabies, distemper, leptospirosis, canine hepatitis, parvovirus, parainfluenza, bordetella, and coronavirus are highly contagious and deadly diseases that have broken many a loving owner's heart in the past. Now that vaccinations are available for these diseases one would think they would no longer be a threat, but many dogs remain unvaccinated and continue to succumb to and spread these potentially fatal illnesses. Don't let your Chihuahua be one of them.

Puppies receive their dam's immunity through nursing in the first day of life. This is why it is important that your pup's mother be properly immunized before breeding, and that your pup be able to nurse from its dam. The immunity gained from the mother will wear off after several weeks, and then the pup will be susceptible to

Healthy adulthood depends upon a good start in life, including proper puppy vaccinations and parasite control.

disease unless you provide immunity through vaccinations. The problem is that there is no way to know exactly when this passive immunity will wear off, and vaccinations given before that time are ineffective. So you must re-vaccinate over a period of weeks so that your pup will not be unprotected and will receive lasting immunity. Your pup's breeder will have given the first vaccinations to your pup before it was old enough to go home with you. Bring all information about your pup's vaccination history to your veterinarian on your first visit so that the pup's vaccination schedule can be maintained. Meanwhile, it is best not to let your pup mingle with strange dogs.

Parasite Control

Intestinal worms: When you take the pup to be vaccinated, bring along a stool specimen so that your veterinarian can also check for worms. Most puppies do have worms at some point, even pups from the most fastidious breeders. This is because some types of worms become encysted in

A Typical Vaccination Schedule

Age (weeks)	Vaccine
6–8	distemper + hepatitis + parainfluenza + parvovirus
10–12	distemper + hepatitis + parainfluenza + parvovirus + leptospirosis
14–16	distemper + hepatitis + parainfluenza + parvovirus + leptospirosis, rabies
18–20	distemper + hepatitis + parainfluenza + parvovirus + leptospirosis

the dam's body long before she ever becomes pregnant; perhaps when she herself is a pup. Here they lie dormant and immune from worming, until hormonal changes due to her pregnancy cause them to be activated, and then they infect her babies. You may be tempted to pick up some worm medication and worm your puppy yourself. Don't. Over-the-counter wormers are largely ineffective and often more dangerous than those available through your veterinarian. Left untreated, worms can cause vomiting, diarrhea, dull coat, listlessness, anemia, and death. Some heartworm preventives also prevent most types of intestinal worms, so that if you have a recurring problem in an older dog, they might help.

Tapeworms tend to plague some dogs throughout their lives. There is no preventive, except to diligently rid your Chihuahua of fleas, because fleas transmit tapeworms to dogs. Tapeworms look like moving white worms on fresh stools, or may dry up and look like rice grains around the dog's anus.

Common Misconceptions about Worms

• Misconception: A dog that is scooting its rear along the ground has worms. This is seldom the case; such a dog more likely has impacted anal sacs.

• Misconception: Feeding a dog sugar and sweets will give it worms. There are good reasons not to feed a dog sweets, but worms have nothing to do with them.

• Misconception: Dogs should be regularly wormed every month or so. Dogs should be wormed when, and only when, they have been diagnosed with worms. No worm medication is completely without risk, and it is foolish to use it carelessly.

Heartworms: Heartworms are a deadly parasite that live in the heart and are carried by mosquitoes. Wherever mosquitoes are present, dogs should be on heartworm preventive. There are several types of heartworm preventive on the market; all are effective. Some are also effective in preventing many other types of worms. Ask your veterinarian when your puppy should begin taking the preventive. If you forget to give the preventive as described, your Chihuahua may get heartworms. A dog with suspected heartworms should not be given the preventive because a fatal reaction could occur. Heartworms are treatable in their early stages, but the treatment is expensive and not without risks. If untreated, heartworms can kill your Chihuahua.

Fleas: A few fleas on a little dog can make its life miserable; a lot of

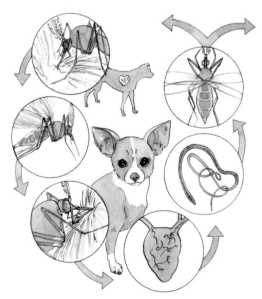

Mosquitoes pass on heartworm larvae from other animals already infected with heartworms. Untreated, these larvae grow and can nearly clog a dog's heart, causing a lot of suffering and eventual death.

fleas can actually be debilitating, causing anemia. They leave behind a black pepperlike substance (actually flea feces) that turns red upon getting wet. Some Chihuahuas develop an allergic reaction to the saliva of the flea; one bite can cause them to itch and chew for days (see How-To: Making Fleas Flee, page 58). Flea allergies are typically characterized by loss of coat and little red bumps around the lower back and tail base.

Ticks: Ticks can carry Rocky Mountain spotted fever, Lyme disease, and, most commonly, "tick fever" (erlichiosis)—all potentially fatal diseases. Use a tissue or tweezers to remove ticks, because some diseases can be transmitted to humans. Grasp the tick as close to the skin as possible, and pull slowly and steadily, trying not to leave the head in the dog. Often a bump will remain after the tick is removed, even if you got the head. It will go away with time.

Ear mites: Tiny but irritating, ear mites are highly contagious and often found in puppies. Affected dogs will shake their head, scratch their ears, and carry their head sideways. There is a dark waxy buildup in the ear canal, usually of both ears. If you place some of this wax on a piece of dark paper, and have very good eyes, you may be able to see tiny white moving specks. These are the culprits. Although there are over-the-counter ear mite preparations, they can cause worse irritation so that ear mites should be diagnosed and treated by your veterinarian.

Mange mites: Dogs are prone to two very different forms of mange. Sarcoptic mange is highly contagious, characterized by intense itching and often scaling of the ear tips, but is easily treated with insecticidal dips. Demodectic mange is not contagious and does not itch, but can be difficult to cure. It tends to run in families, and is characterized by a moth-eaten appearance, often on the face or feet; advanced cases lead to serious secondary infections. Some localized forms may go away on their own, but more widespread cases will need a special dip regime prescribed by your veterinarian. You must adhere to the dip schedule fanatically in order to effect a cure in these cases. Chihuahuas are a breed that seems to be at risk for demodectic mange.

Dental Care

At around five to six months of age, your Chihuahua puppy will begin to shed its baby teeth and show off new permanent teeth. Often baby teeth, especially the canines, are not shed, so that the permanent tooth grows in beside the baby tooth. If this condition persists for over a week, consult your veterinarian. Retained baby teeth can cause misalignment of adult teeth.

Check the way your puppy's teeth meet up; in a correct bite, the bottom incisors should touch the back of the top incisors when the mouth is closed. Deviations from this can cause

Examine your Chihuahua's teeth regularly beginning at a young age.

Good health is evident in these adults' alert and curious expressions, with faces free of discharges and blemishes.

chewing problems and discomfort. Overshot, undershot, and wry bites are common problems in Chihuahuas. Most Chihuahuas have full dentition, but it is not uncommon for some to be missing their canine teeth. Never remove puppy teeth unless a permanent tooth is clearly present.

As your dog gets older, its teeth will tend to accumulate plaque. The plaque can be removed by brushing the dog's teeth once or twice weekly with a child's toothbrush and doggy toothpaste. You can also rub the teeth with hydrogen peroxide or a baking soda solution on a gauze pad to help remove tartar. Hard dog foods and chew bones are helpful, but cannot do the job on their own. If not removed, plaque will attract bacteria and minerals, which will harden into tartar. If you cannot brush, your veterinarian can supply cleansing solution that will help

to kill plaque-forming bacteria, as well as bad breath! Neglected plaque and tartar can cause infections to form along the gum line. The infection can gradually work its way down the sides of the tooth until the entire root is undermined. The tissues and bone around the tooth erode, and the tooth finally falls out. Meanwhile, the bacteria may have been picked up by the bloodstream and carried throughout the body, causing infection in the kidneys and heart valves. Thicker tartar deposits will have to be removed with a dental scraper, possibly under anesthesia, which entails some risk in older Chihuahuas.

Small dogs are especially prone to tooth loss and periodontal disease. There is no such thing as doggy dentures, so help your Chihuahua keep its teeth into old age by keeping its teeth sparkling throughout its life.

The proper Chihuahua gait is free-stepping and sound. Limping, hopping for a step, or moving bow-legged could indicate a disorder such as patellar luxation.

Common Ailments and Symptoms

Coughing: Any persistent cough should be checked by your veterinarian. Coughing irritates the throat and can lead to secondary infections if allowed to continue unchecked. There are many reasons for coughing, including allergies, but two of the most common are kennel cough and heart disease.

Kennel cough is a highly communicable airborne disease against which you can also request your dog be vaccinated. This is an especially good idea if you plan to have your dog around other dogs at training classes or while being boarded.

Heart disease can result in coughing following exercise or in the evening. Treatment with diuretics prescribed by your veterinarian can help alleviate the coughing for awhile.

Chihuahuas are subject to pulmonic stenosis and mitral valve defects, both of which can cause circulatory problems and may have a genetic basis.

Coughing may also result from a collapsed trachea. In these dogs the rings of the trachea are not formed correctly, and with increasing age and weight, the upper part of the trachea may collapse inward. This may cause a chronic "honking" cough and difficulty breathing. The condition can be treated with medicine or surgery.

Vomiting: Vomiting is a common occurrence that may or may not indicate a serious problem. You should consult your veterinarian immediately if your dog vomits a foul substance resembling fecal matter (indicating a blockage in the intestinal tract), blood (partially digested blood resembles coffee grounds), or if there is projectile vomiting, in which the stomach contents are forcibly ejected up to a distance of several feet. Sporadic vomiting with poor appetite and generally poor condition could indicate worms or a more serious internal disease that should also be checked by your veterinarian.

Overeating is a common cause of vomiting in puppies, especially if they follow eating with playing. Feed smaller meals more frequently if this becomes a problem. Vomiting after eating grass is common and usually of no great concern. Repeated vomiting could indicate that the dog has eaten spoiled food, undigestible objects, or may have stomach illness. Use the same home treatment as that outlined for diarrhea below.

Diarrhea: Diarrhea can result from overexcitement or nervousness, a change in diet or water, sensitivity to certain foods, overeating, intestinal parasites, infectious diseases such as parvovirus or coronavirus, or ingestion of toxic substances. Bloody diarrhea, diarrhea with vomiting, fever, or other signs of toxicity, or diarrhea that lasts for more than a day should not be allowed to continue without veterinary advice.

Less severe diarrhea can be treated at home by withholding or severely restricting food and water. Ice cubes can be given to satisfy thirst. Administer a human antidiarrheal medicine in the same weight dosage as recommended for humans. A bland diet consisting of rice (flavored if need be with cooked, drained hamburger), cottage cheese, or cooked macaroni should be given for several days.

Urinary tract diseases: If your dog drinks and urinates more than usual, it may be suffering from a kidney problem. See your veterinarian for a proper diagnosis and treatment. Although the excessive urination may cause problems in keeping your house clean or your night's sleep intact, *never* try to restrict water from a dog

with kidney disease. Untreated kidney disease can lead to death. Increased thirst and urination could also be a sign of diabetes.

If your dog has difficulty or pain in urination, urinates suddenly but in small amounts, or passes cloudy or bloody urine, it may be suffering from a problem of the bladder, urethra, or prostate. Your veterinarian will need to examine your Chihuahua to determine the exact nature of the problem. Bladder infections must be treated promptly to avoid the infection reaching the kidneys. A common cause of urinary incontinence in older spayed females is lack of estrogen, which can be treated. Your veterinarian should check your older male's prostate to ensure that it is not overly enlarged, which can cause problems in both urination and defecation.

Impacted anal sacs: Dogs have two anal sacs that are normally emptied by rectal pressure during defecation. Their musky smelling contents may also be forcibly ejected when a dog is extremely frightened. Sometimes they fail to empty properly and become impacted or infected. This is more common in small dogs, obese dogs, dogs with seborrhea, and dogs that seldom have firm stools. Constant licking of the anus or scooting of the anus along the ground are characteristic signs of anal sac impaction. Not only is this an extremely uncomfortable condition for your dog, but left unattended, the impacted sacs can become infected. Your veterinarian can show you how to empty the anal sacs yourself. Some dogs may never need to have their anal sacs expressed, but others may need regular attention.

Eye discharge: A watery discharge, accompanied by squinting or pawing, often indicates a foreign body in the eye. Examine under the lids and use a moist cotton swab to remove any debris. Flooding the eye with saline solution can also aid in removal. Continued tearing of the eye could be due to eyelid anomalies that irritate the cornea; if ignored, they could injure the eye to the point of causing blindness.

A thick or crusty discharge suggests conjunctivitis. Mild cases can be treated by over-the-counter preparations for humans, but if you don't see improvement within a day of treatment, your veterinarian should be consulted.

Keratitis sicca (dry eye) is a condition to which Chihuahuas are prone. There is inadequate tear production, resulting in irritation to the surface of the eye whenever the dog blinks. If you look at the surface of the eye, it may appear dull; you may also see a thick mucous discharge from the eye. Left untreated, the condition is extremely painful and can lead to blindness.

Secondary glaucoma is also more prevalent in Chihuahuas than in some other breeds. Glaucoma is an elevation of the fluid pressure within the eye, and can result from a number of different causes. Unfortunately, it may be hard to detect and can do its damage rapidly. The dog may rub at its eye, avoid bright light, have excessive tear stain, and display reddened whites of its eyes. In more advanced cases, the pupil will be enlarged and unreactive to light, the eye surface may become cloudy, and the entire eye may be enlarged. This condition calls for immediate veterinary attention.

Any time your dog's pupils do not react to light or when one eye reacts differently from another, take it to the veterinarian immediately. It could indicate a serious ocular or neurological problem.

Skin and coat problems: Itchy skin most often results from flea infestation, sarcoptic mange, or allergies (to food, airborne particles, grass, or flea saliva). First make sure that not a single flea is on your dog. If scratching continues, you and your veterinarian will have to play detectives. Mange mites can be detected through skin scrapings; for allergies, you can try avoiding certain foods and environments. Often a lamb and rice-based food will bring relief. New carpeting or wet grass may be the culprit. Cortisone can bring some relief from the itching, but can cause damage to your Chihuahua in the long run if used too frequently.

In some cases, hair is lost without the dog itching. Demodectic mange, thyroid deficiency, adrenal gland disease, estrogen excess, ringworm, and seborrhea are all possibilities that your veterinarian can diagnose.

Blisters and brown crust on the stomach of your puppy indicate puppy impetigo. Clean the area twice daily with dilute hydrogen peroxide or surgical soap, and treat with a topical antibiotic.

Most bumps and lumps are not cause for concern, but because there is always a possibility of cancer, they should be examined by your veterinarian. This is especially true of a sore that does not heal, or any pigmented lump that begins to grow or bleed.

Limping: Puppies are especially susceptible to bone and joint injuries, and should not be encouraged to jump off of high places, walk on their hind legs, or run until exhausted. Persistent limping in puppies may result from one of several developmental bone problems, and should be checked. Both puppies and adults should be kept off of slippery floors that could cause them to lose their footing. Limping may or may not indicate a serious problem. When associated with extreme pain, fever, swelling, discoloration, deformity, or grinding or popping sounds, you should have your veterinarian

These housemates illustrate the different phases of the Chihuahua's lifetime: the boundless energy of youth, the calm self-reliance of adulthood, and the sedate wisdom of age.

examine your Chihuahua at once. Ice packs may help minimize swelling if applied immediately after an injury. Fractures should be immobilized by splinting above and below the site of fracture (small rolled magazines work well on legs) before moving the dog. Mild lameness should be treated by complete rest; if it still persists after three days, your dog will need to be examined by its doctor. Knee injuries are common in dogs; most do not get well on their own. Avoid pain medications that might encourage the use of an injured limb. In older dogs, or dogs with a previous injury, limping is often the result of arthritis. Arthritis can be treated with aspirin, but should be done so only under veterinary supervision. Do not use ibuprofen or naxo-

pren. Toy breeds are more prone to be affected with rheumatoid arthritis. Any time a young or middle-aged dog shows signs of arthritis, especially in a joint that has not been previously injured, it should be examined by its veterinarian.

Chihuahuas are prone to patellar luxation (displaced kneecap), especially when they are young. In most dogs, the patella is held in its proper position by a deep groove, but in many Chihuahuas, the groove is too shallow. In these dogs, you can actually push the patella out of place to either the inside or outside of the knee. When out of place, the dog cannot straighten its leg and will tend to hold the affected leg up for a few steps at a time, or all of the time, until the patella pops back

All chihuahuas appreciate having a special spot in the sun.

into place. While standing, it may appear either knock-kneed or bow-legged. This condition can be surgically repaired; if it is present in a puppy, such repair should be done by a few months of age, before the leg becomes permanently deformed.

Medications

Giving medications to your Chihuahua should not be difficult. For pills, open your dog's mouth and place (don't throw) the pill well to the back and in the middle of the tongue. Close the mouth and gently stroke the throat until your dog swallows. Pre-wetting capsules or covering them with cream cheese or some other food helps prevent capsules from sticking to the tongue or the roof of the mouth. For liquid medicine, tilt the head back and place the liquid in the pouch of the cheek. Then close your dog's mouth until it swallows. Always give the full course of medications prescribed by your veterinarian.

You may also need to take your dog's temperature on occasion. Use a rectal thermometer, preferably the digital type; lubricate it, and insert it about 1.5 inches (3.8 cm). Do not allow your dog to sit down, or the thermometer could break. Normal temperature for a small dog is around 102°F (38.9°C). Incidentally, not only do small dogs tend to have a slightly higher body temperature than do large dogs, but they also tend to have a higher heart rate, averaging about 180 beats per minute (200 to 220 per minute for puppies).

HOW-TO:
Dealing with Emergencies

Deciding whether or not you have an emergency can sometimes be difficult. What would not be an emergency for the average dog may very well be an emergency for a Chihuahua. The following situations are all *life-threatening emergencies*. For all cases, administer the first aid treatment outlined and seek the nearest veterinary help *immediately*. Call the clinic first so that they can prepare.

In General
• Make sure breathing passages are open. Loosen the collar and check mouth and throat.
• Be calm and reassuring. A calm dog is less likely to go into shock.
• Move the dog as little and as gently as possible.
• If the dog is in pain, it may bite. Apply a makeshift muzzle with a bandage, shoelace, or tape. Do not muzzle if breathing difficulties are present.

Shock
Signs: Very pale gums, weakness, unresponsiveness, faint pulse, shivering.

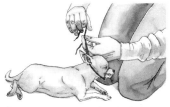

An emergency muzzle can be fashioned from a shoelace.

Treatment: Keep the dog warm and calm; control any bleeding; check breathing, pulse, and consciousness, and treat these problems if needed.

Heatstroke
Signs: Rapid, loud breathing; abundant thick saliva, bright red mucous membranes, high rectal temperature. Later signs: unsteadiness, diarrhea, coma.
Treatment: Immediately wrap the dog in towels soaked in cold water and place the dog in front of a fan or in a cold environment. A less preferred method is to immerse the dog in cold water. You *must* lower your dog's body temperature quickly (but do not lower it below 100°F [37.8°C]).

Cool a heatstroke victim with a towel soaked in cold water.

Breathing Difficulties
Signs: Gasping for breath with head extended, anxiety, weakness; advances to loss of consciousness, bluish tongue (exception: carbon monoxide poisoning causes bright red tongue).
Treatment: If not breathing, give mouth-to-nose respiration:
1. Open the dog's mouth; clear passage of secretions and foreign bodies.
2. Pull the dog's tongue forward.

3. Seal your mouth over dog's nose and mouth; blow gently into the dog's nose for three seconds, then release.
4. Continue until your dog breathes on its own.

If due to drowning, turn your dog upside down, holding it by the hind legs, so that water can run out of its mouth. Then administer mouth-to-nose respiration, with the dog's head positioned lower than its lungs.

Hypoglycemia (Low Blood Sugar)
Signs: Appears disoriented, weak, staggering. May appear blind, and muscles may twitch. Later stages lead to convulsions, coma, and death.
Treatment: Give food, or honey or syrup mixed with warm water.

Poisoning
Signs: Varies according to poison, but commonly include vomiting, convulsions, staggering, collapse
Treatment: Call your veterinarian and give as much information as possible. Induce vomiting (*except* in the cases outlined below) by giving either hydrogen peroxide, salt water, or mustard and water. Treat for shock and get to the veterinarian at once. Be prepared for convulsions or respiratory distress.

Do *not* induce vomiting if the poison was an acid, alkali, petroleum product, solvent, cleaner, or tranquilizer, or if a sharp object was swallowed; also do *not* induce vomiting if the dog is severely depressed, convulsing, comatose, or if over two hours have passed since ingestion. If the dog is *not* convulsing or unconscious: dilute the poison by giving milk, vegetable oil, or egg whites.

Convulsions
Signs: Drooling, stiffness, muscle spasms.

Treatment: Prevent your dog from injuring itself on furniture or stairs. Remove other dogs from the area. Treat for shock.

Snakebites
Signs: Swelling, discoloration, pain, fang marks, restlessness, nausea, weakness.

Treatment: Restrain the dog and keep it quiet. Be able to describe the snake. If you can't get to the veterinarian, apply a tourniquet between the bite and the heart tight enough to prevent blood from returning to the heart. Make vertical parallel cuts (deep enough for blood to ooze out of) through the fang marks and suction out the blood (do not use your mouth if you have any open sores).

Open Wounds
Signs: Consider wounds to be an emergency if there is profuse bleeding, if extremely deep, if open to chest cavity, abdominal cavity, or head.

Treatment: Control massive bleeding first. Cover the wound with a clean dressing and apply pressure; apply more dressings over the others until bleeding stops. Also elevate the wound site, and apply a cold pack to the site. If an extremity, apply pressure to the closest pressure point as follows:
• For a front leg: inside of the front leg just above the elbow.
• For a rear leg: inside of the thigh where the femoral artery crosses the thighbone.
• For the tail: underside of the tail close to where it joins the body.

Use a tourniquet only in life-threatening situations and when all other attempts have failed. Check for signs of shock.

Sucking chest wounds: Place a sheet of plastic or other nonporous material over the hole and bandage it to make an airtight seal.

Abdominal wounds: Place warm wet sterile dressing over any protruding internal organs; cover with a bandage or towel. Do not attempt to push organs back into the dog.

Head wounds: Apply gentle pressure to control bleeding. Monitor for loss of consciousness or shock, and treat accordingly.

Deep Burns
Signs: Charred or pearly white skin; deeper layers of tissue exposed.

Treatment: Cool burned area with cool packs, towels soaked in ice water, or by immersing in cold water. If over 50 percent of the dog is burned, do not immerse as this increases the likelihood of shock. Cover with a clean bandage or towel to avoid contamination. Do not apply pressure; do not apply ointments. Monitor for shock.

Electrical Shock
Signs: Collapse, burns inside mouth.

Treatment: Before touching the dog, disconnect the plug or cut power; if that cannot be done immediately, use a wooden pencil, spoon, or broom handle to knock the cord away from the

Maintain an emergency kit for your Chihuahua, and keep it stocked at all times.

dog. Keep your dog warm and treat for shock. Monitor breathing and heartbeat.

Prolapsed Eyeball
Signs: Eyeball partially or entirely popped out of socket, often following a blow to the head.

Treatment: Cover the eye with a dampened sponge or soft cloth. See if the eye will slip back into the socket but do not further traumatize it.

Again, the procedures outlined above are first aid only. They do not take the place of the emergency veterinary clinic. Nor is the above list a complete catalog of emergency situations. Situations not described can usually be treated with the same first aid as for humans.

You should maintain a first aid/medical kit for your Chihuahua, which should contain at least: rectal thermometer, scissors, tweezers, sterile gauze dressings, self-adhesive bandage, instant cold compress, antidiarrhea medication, ophthalmic ointment, soap, antiseptic skin ointment, hydrogen peroxide, first aid instructions, and veterinarian and emergency clinic numbers.

Reflecting years of good care, a veteran long-coated Chihuahua boasts a fully mature coat and tail plume.

The Older Chihuahua

Chihuahua owners are among the most fortunate of dog owners because of the renowned Chihuahua longevity. As your Chihuahua ages, you may first notice that it sleeps longer and more soundly than it did as a youngster. Upon awakening, it is slower to get going and may be stiff at first. It may be less eager to play and more content to lie in the sun. Some dogs become cranky and less patient, especially when dealing with puppies or boisterous children.

Older dogs may seem to ignore their owners' commands, but this may be the result of hearing loss. The slight haziness that appears in the older dog's pupils is normal and has minimal effect upon vision, but some dogs, especially those with diabetes, may develop cataracts. These can be removed by a veterinary ophthalmologist if they are severe.

Both physical activity and metabolic rates decrease in older animals, meaning that they require fewer calories to maintain the same weight. It is important to keep your older dog active. Older dogs that are continued to be fed the same as when they were young risk becoming obese; such dogs have a greater risk of cardiovascular and joint problems.

Older dogs should be fed several small meals instead of one large meal, and should be fed on time. There are a variety of reduced calorie, low protein senior diets on the market. But most older dogs do not require a special diet unless they have a particular medical need for it (e.g., obesity: low calorie; kidney failure: low protein; heart failure: low sodium). Dogs with these problems may require special prescription dog foods that better address their needs.

Like people, dogs lose skin moisture as they age, and though dogs don't wrinkle, their skin can become dry and itchy as a result. Regular brushing can stimulate oil production. Older dogs tend to have a stronger body odor, but don't just ignore increased odors. They could indicate specific problems, such as periodontal disease, impacted anal sacs, seborrhea, ear infections, or even kidney disease. Any strong odor should be checked by your veterinarian.

There is evidence that the immune system may be less effective in older dogs. This means that it is increasingly important to shield your dog from infectious disease, chilling, overheating, and any stressful conditions. Older dogs present a somewhat greater anesthesia risk. Most of this increased risk can be negated, however, by first screening dogs with a complete medical workup, which may include bloodwork, radiographs, or an EKG.

Long trips may be grueling, and boarding in a kennel may be extremely upsetting. Introduction of a puppy or new pet may be welcomed and may encourage your older dog to play, but if your dog is not used to other dogs, the newcomer will more likely be resented and be an additional source of stress.

The older dog should see its veterinarian at least biyearly, but the owner must take responsibility for observing any health changes. Some of the more common changes, along with some of the more common conditions they may indicate in older dogs, are:
• Limping: arthritis, patellar luxation.
• Nasal discharge: tumor, periodontal disease.
• Coughing: heart disease, tracheal collapse, lung cancer.
• Difficulty eating: periodontal disease, oral tumors.
• Decreased appetite: kidney, liver, or heart disease, pancreatitis, cancer.
• Increased appetite: diabetes, Cushing's syndrome.
• Weight loss: heart, liver, or kidney disease, diabetes, cancer

Older dogs enjoy the companionship of other Chihuahuas.

• Abdominal distension: heart or kidney disease, Cushing's syndrome, tumor.
• Increased urination: diabetes, kidney or liver disease, cystitis, Cushing's syndrome.
• Diarrhea: kidney or liver disease, pancreatitis.

The above list is by no means inclusive of all symptoms or problems they may indicate. Vomiting and diarrhea can signal many different problems; keep in mind that a small older dog cannot tolerate the dehydration that results from continued vomiting or diarrhea and you should not let it continue unchecked.

In general, any ailment that an older dog has is magnified in severity compared to the same symptoms in a younger dog. The owner of any older dog must be even more careful and attentive as his or her dog ages. Don't be lulled into a false sense of security just because you own a Chihuahua. A long life depends upon good genes, good care, and good luck.

The Chihuahua Companion

Owning a Chihuahua means having a friend who is never critical or judgmental, who always greets you with glee, and who is always willing to cuddle on lonely evenings and frolic on sunny afternoons. A dog is also motivation to get out of the house, and is a good catalyst for meeting other people. Chihuahuas can bring joy into your life; have you ever thought of sharing?

Sharing Your Chihuahua

As more of the population becomes elderly and either unable to care for or keep a pet, the result is particularly sad for lonely people who may have relied upon the companionship of a

Chihuahuas can bring love to the lives of people who do not have families.

pet throughout most of their independent years. Studies have shown that pet ownership increases life expectancy and petting animals can lower blood pressure. In recent years, nursing home residents have come to look forward to visits by dogs, particularly Chihuahuas. These dogs must be meticulously well mannered and well groomed; to be registered as a Certified Therapy Dog a dog must demonstrate that it will act in an obedient, outgoing, gentle manner to strangers. A friendly little Chihuahua could make a big difference in an elderly person's day.

For Better or Worse

Even if you can't share your Chihuahua with others, you will be sharing your life with your pet. Both of you will change through the years. Accept that your Chihuahua will change as it matures: from the cute, eager to please baby, to the cute, mischievous, often disobedient adolescent, then to the self-reliant adult partner, and finally the proud but frail senior. Be sure that you remember the promise you made to yourself and your future puppy before you made the commitment to share your life: to keep your interest in your dog and care for it everyday of its life with as much love and enthusiasm as you did the first day it arrived home.

Irreconcilable Differences

Sometimes relationships just don't work out. If you absolutely find that you do not like your dog, perhaps it is best to find it a new loving home, rather than to grudgingly put up with it for years. If your dog has behavioral problems, talk to your veterinarian and explore what alternatives are possible. Remember that few other families will want a dog with problems. But if it is simply a case of irreconcilable differences, contact the Chihuahua rescue organization.

Till Death Do Us Part

Unfortunately there comes the time when, no matter how diligent you have been, neither you nor your veterinarian can prevent your Chihuahua from succumbing to old age or an incurable illness. It seems hard to believe that you will have to say good-bye to someone who has been such a focal point of your life; in truth, a real member of your family. That dogs live such a short time compared to humans is a cruel fact, and as much as you may wish otherwise, your Chihuahua is a dog and is not immortal.

You should realize that both of you have been fortunate to have shared so many good times, but make sure that your Chihuahua's remaining time is still pleasurable. Many terminal illnesses make your dog feel very bad, and there comes a point where your desire to keep your friend with you as long as possible may not be the kindest thing for either of you. Ask your veterinarian if there is a reasonable chance of your dog getting better, and if it is likely your dog is suffering. Ask yourself if your pet is getting pleasure out of life, and if it enjoys most of its days. If your Chihuahua no longer eats its dinner or treats, this is a sign that it does not feel well and you must face the prospect of doing what is best for your beloved friend. Euthanasia is painless and involves giving an overdose of an anesthetic. If your dog is scared of the vet's office,

you might feel better having the doctor meet you at home or come out to your car. Although it won't be easy, try to remain with your Chihuahua so that its last moments will be filled with your love; otherwise have a friend that your dog knows stay with your dog. Try to recall the wonderful times you have shared and realize that however painful losing such a once-in-a-lifetime dog is, it is better than never having had such a friend in the first place.

Many people who regarded their pet as a member of the family nonetheless feel embarrassed at the grief they feel at its loss. Yet this dog has often functioned as a surrogate child, best friend, and confidant. Everyone should be lucky enough to find a human with the faithful and loving qualities of their dogs. In some ways, the loss of a pet can be harder than that of more distant family members, especially because the support from friends that comes with human loss is too often absent with pet loss. Such well-meaning but ill-informed statements as "he was just a dog" or "just get another one" do little to ease the pain, but the truth is that many people simply don't know how to react and probably aren't really as callous as they might sound. There are, however, many people who share your feelings and there are pet bereavement counselors available at many veterinary schools.

After losing such a dog, many people say they will never get another. True, no dog will ever take the place of your dog. But you will find that another dog is a welcome diversion and will help keep you from dwelling on the loss of your first pet, as long as you don't keep comparing the new dog to the old. True also, by getting another dog you are sentencing yourself to the same grief in another 10 to 15 years, but wouldn't you rather have that than miss out on all of the love and companionship altogether?

Chihuahuas make delightful friends for people of all ages.

As Momma's little helpers, Chihuahuas are a never-ending source of amusement when it comes to household chores.

Chihuahua Nutrition

Little dogs entail big feeding responsibilities. And little dogs fall victim to poor feeding practices far too often. Why? Because little dogs don't need much food. If a little dog gets a lot of food, it will no longer be a little dog. So if you sneak your Chihuahua a few potato chips and the remains of your ice cream—a mere morsel for most dogs—your Chihuahua will have very little room left for its properly balanced dog food. Add to this the Chihuahua's demanding nature and hungry eyes, and a decided tendency for Chihuahua owners to dote on their dears, and you have a recipe for poor nutrition and obesity.

The Chubby Chihuahua

Very young puppies should be fed three or four times a day, on a regular schedule. Feed them as much as they care to eat in about 15 minutes. From the age of three to six months, pups should be fed three times daily, and after that, twice daily. Adult dogs can be fed once a day, but it is actually preferable to feed smaller meals twice a day. Some people let the dog decide when to eat by leaving dry food available at all times. If you choose to let the dog "self-feed," monitor its weight to be sure it is not overindulging.

Proper Chihuahua weight will depend upon the bone structure of the dog. The so-called "pocket-sized" Chihuahuas weigh less than 3 pounds (1.4 kg); a small Chihuahua weighs about 4 pounds (1.8 kg), and the AKC standard dictates that no proper-sized Chihuahua should weigh over 6 pounds (2.7 kg). You should be able to just feel the ribs slightly when you run your hands along the rib cage, and there should be an indication of a waistline, both when viewed from above and from the side. There should not be a dimple at the tail base. If your Chihuahua is overweight, try a less fattening food or feed less of your current food; make sure family members aren't sneaking it tidbits. If your Chihuahua remains overweight, seek your veterinarian's opinion. Some endocrine disorders, such as hypothyroidism or Cushing's disease can cause the appearance of obesity and should be ruled out or treated. Little Chihuahua legs were not meant to support round ticklike bodies; obese Chihuahuas miss out on a lot of fun in

Fat Chihuahuas, with overgrown toenails, are seen far too often. Their owners are "killing them with love."

life, and are prone to joint injuries, tracheal collapse, chronic bronchitis, and a shortened life span.

Several commercial high-fiber, low-fat and low-protein diet dog foods are available, which supply about 15 percent fewer calories per pound. It is preferable to feed one of these foods rather than simply feeding less of a high-calorie food. Special care must be taken when putting small dogs on a diet, because they have a high metabolic rate and dissipate heat easily. They cannot store sufficient body fat to endure long periods of food restriction, especially in cold weather. Don't try for overnight results.

The Choosy Chihuahua

Finicky eaters and skinny Chihuahuas are another special challenge. Many picky eaters are created when their owners begin to spice up their food with especially tasty treats. The dog then refuses to eat unless the preferred treat is offered, and finally learns that if it refuses even that proffered treat, another even tastier enticement will be offered. Give your Chihuahua a good, tasty meal, but don't succumb to Chihuahua blackmail or you may be a slave to your dog's gastronomical whims for years to come. If you do have an underweight dog, try feeding puppy food; add water, milk, or canned food and heat slightly to increase aroma and palatability.

Chihuahua Chow

There are a number of high-quality palatable foods on the market from which to choose, but one of your first choices will be which form of food to feed: dry, moist, or canned. Dry food is the most popular, economical, and healthiest, but least palatable. The high moisture content of canned foods helps to make them tasty, but it also makes them comparatively expensive, because you are in essence buying

Dry dog food is popular, economical, and healthy, but also the least tasty of the three forms available.

water. A steady diet of canned food would not provide the chewing necessary to maintain dental health. In addition, a high meat content, such as often found in canned foods, tends to increase levels of dental plaque. Moist foods are popular with some dog owners, but these too cannot provide proper chewing and also have the disadvantage of being fairly expensive and loaded with preservatives. But many dogs enjoy them so they can be a reasonable choice for use in conjunction with a high-quality dry food. They are also very convenient when traveling. Dog biscuits provide excellent chewing action, and some of the better varieties provide complete nutrition.

The Fine Print

When comparing food labels, keep in mind that differences in moisture content make it virtually impossible to make comparisons between the guaranteed analyses in different forms of food. The components that vary most from one brand of food to another are protein and fat percentages.

Protein: Many high-quality foods boast of being high in protein, and with good reason. Protein provides the necessary building blocks for growth and maintenance of bones and muscle, and in the production of infection-fighting antibodies. The best sources of protein are meat based, but soybeans are also a popular source. Puppies and adolescents need particularly high protein levels in their diets, which is one reason they are best fed a food formulated for their life stage. Older dogs, especially those with kidney problems, should be fed much lower levels of very high-quality protein.

Fat: Fat is the calorie-rich component of foods, and most dogs prefer the taste of foods with higher fat content. Fat is necessary to good health, aiding in the transport of important vitamins and providing energy. Dogs deficient in

When choosing the best dog food to use, you will probably have to reach a compromise with your Chihuahua, since your pet will go for flavor and you want nutrition.

Dogs find canned food the tastiest food available, but owners find it the most expensive.

fat often have sparse, dry coats. A higher fat content is usually found in puppy foods, whereas obese dogs or dogs with heart problems would do well to be fed a lower fat food.

Choose a food that has a protein and fat content best suited for your dog's life stage, adjusting for any weight or health problems (there are a number of special diets available from your veterinarian especially designed for specific health problems). Also examine the list of ingredients: A good rule of thumb is that three or four of the first six ingredients should be animal derived. These tend to be more palatable and more highly digestible than plant-based ingredients; more highly digestible foods mean less stool volume and less gas problems.

Your Chihuahua, of course, will make the final decision about what food is acceptable, but some compromising may be in order. Find a food that your dog likes, one that creates a small volume of firm stools and results in good weight with a nice coat. Be aware of the signs of possible food allergies (loss of hair, scratching, inflamed ears). You may have to do a

little experimenting to find just the right food, but a word of warning: One of the great mysteries of life is why a species, such as the dog, that is renown for its lead stomach and preference to eat out of garbage cans, can at the same time develop violently upset stomachs simply from changing from one high-quality dog food to another. But it happens. So when changing foods you should do so gradually, mixing in progressively more and more of the new food each day for several days.

Never Feed
• Any small bones, but especially chicken or fish bones. These can be swallowed and their sharp ends can pierce the stomach or intestinal walls.
 • Any bone that could be swallowed whole. This could cause choking or intestinal blockage.
• Mineral supplements unless advised to do so by your veterinarian.
• Chocolate. Contains theobromine, which is poisonous to dogs.
• Alcohol. Small dogs can drink fatal amounts quickly.
• Raw meat.

A Chihuahua with its own idea about mealtime!

Is it dinner, or is it actually a being <u>smaller</u> than a Chihuahua?

Breeding Champion Chihuahuas

Why You *Don't* Want to Breed

Most people who breed their Chihuahuas are doing their pets, the breed, and the resulting puppies a world of disservice. There are more reasons *not* to breed a litter than there are to breed one:

• A spayed female is less likely to develop breast cancer and a number of other hormone-related diseases. She should be spayed before her first season in order to avoid these problems.

• There is definite discomfort and a certain amount of danger to any dog, but especially a tiny dog, when whelping a litter. Watching a litter be born is not a good way to teach the children the miracle of life; there are too many things that can go wrong.

• A litter is expensive! Stud fee, prenatal care, whelping complications, cesarean sections, supplemental feeding, puppy food, vaccinations, advertising, and a staggering investment of time and energy should be considered.

• Serious breeders have spent years researching genetics and the breed; they breed only the best specimens and screen for hereditary defects in order to obtain superior puppies. Until you have done the same, you are undoing the hard work of those who have dedicated their lives to bettering the breed.

• Finding responsible buyers is very difficult, and you may end up feeling like the warden at a home for delinquent jumping beans. You may find homes, but will they really be good homes?

• There are many more purebred Chihuahuas in the world than there are good homes for them. The puppy you sell to a less-than-perfect buyer may end up neglected or discarded, or used to produce puppies to sell to even less desirable homes. Millions of purebreds are euthanized each year at pounds. Sometimes they are the lucky ones.

Prospective Chihuahua breeders have one more worry than do breeders of most other dogs. All Chihuahuas are little; some Chihuahuas are tiny. Tiny Chihuahua females (under 3 pounds [1.4 kg]) are simply physically too small to breed safely. Even if bred to a tiny stud, there is a definite risk that

A healthy, good-quality litter requires a lot of work and planning, and typically results in very few pups.

any resulting puppies would be too large to be carried full term, or to be whelped naturally. Cherish your tiny Chihuahua female, but don't risk her life by breeding her.

Why do otherwise sane people breed dogs at all? Ethical and knowledgeable breeders seldom do. They breed a litter only after studying the breed standard, pedigrees, and individual dogs to find the most advantageous match of conformation, temperament, and health. Then, after proving the worth of both prospective parents through competitions, they find a number of responsible buyers. They have money set aside for prenatal and postnatal care, and emergency funds and vacation time available for whelping or postwhelping complications. They have the commitment to keep every single puppy born for the rest of its life should good homes not be available or should they ever have to be returned. And they worry a lot. Is it any wonder that some of the best breeders breed the least? When they do breed, it is because they love the Chihuahua, and they believe that their puppies could be a worthwhile addition not only to the breed, but to somebody's life.

If You Must Breed

If you still have not been dissuaded from breeding your Chihuahua, at least do it the right way. A litter will entail a lot of sacrifice on your part. You owe it to yourself to settle for no less than the best available Chihuahua stud. Look for a stud that is superior in the areas your bitch needs improvement. Look for a stud owner who is honest about his or her dog's faults, health problems, and temperament. You want someone who is trustworthy, dependable, and experienced in breeding. A responsible stud owner will have proven the stud by earning titles, will have complete records and photos of

other litters the stud has produced, and will insist that your bitch and her pedigree be compatible before accepting her for breeding.

The Pedigree

Once you have narrowed your list to several potential studs, you will want to consider their pedigrees. The pedigree is more than just a list of strange names that you can trot out to impress your friends. It is a history of breeding decisions that can predict how your litter may look, so you should try to obtain pictures or descriptions of the dogs in it. The pedigree can also tell you how closely related the prospective sire and dam are.

Inbreeding refers to a system of mating that makes it more likely that an offspring will inherit identical copies of the same gene from both its mother and father. The problem with inbreeding lies in the fact that the majority of serious hereditary defects are recessive in nature, meaning that two identical copies of the gene for that defect must be inherited for the trait to be expressed—exactly what inbreeding promotes! Unless there is a specific reason to inbreed, and you have a firm grasp of the genetic principles involved, and are intimately familiar with the dogs in the pedigree, such close breeding is not advisable.

Linebreeding refers to the situation when there is one name that appears over and over in the pedigree, indicating a concerted effort to intensify the genetic influence of a particular individual. Such a breeding will also be somewhat inbred, and carries the same caveat (though usually to a lesser degree) as does inbreeding.

Outcrossing is the mating of individuals sharing no common ancestors in the pedigree. This is generally the safest way to go, but has the shortcoming that the results are less predictable.

Chihuahua Genetics

Before you take the final step, you owe it to yourself to understand the genetics of the Chihuahua. After all, if you are breeding in hopes of getting a certain color and coat type, for instance, you need to know if your prospective parents are even capable of producing it.

Dogs have 78 pairs of chromosomes, each containing sequences of DNA that direct cells to develop in certain ways, or genes. In each pair there are two sets of alternate genes, known as alleles: one inherited from the sire, the other from the dam. If the two alleles are not alike, one allele (the dominant one) may mask the presence of the other (recessive) one, or the result may be a mix of the two alleles' influence.

Not all traits are passed in this simple "dominant/recessive" nature. Many are the result of many, many pairs of alleles all working together to produce subtle degrees of variation. Size is an example of such "polygenic" inheritance; a large Chihuahua bred to a small one would more likely have offspring intermediate in size, although there would be considerable variation in what size the offspring actually would be. There are still many traits for which the genetic aspects are not yet understood; when in doubt, the best thing to do is to avoid breeding dogs with similar faults.

Smooth vs. long coat: The genetics of smooth coat versus long coat are fairly simple, and will provide a good example with which to set forth the basics of genetic principles.

In Chihuahuas, one dominant gene controls whether the coat will be short. If a Chihuahua has an allele for short coat (C) and one for long coat (c), then that individual would have a short coat. A short-coated Chihuahua could have either both alleles the same (C/C) or they could be different (C/c),

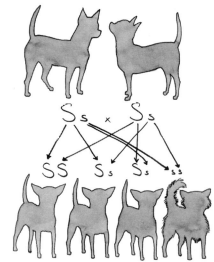

Two smooth coats that carry recessive genes for long coats will on average produce a litter in which one quarter of the pups receive two recessive genes and so are long coats.

but a long-coated Chihuahua could have only both alleles alike (c/c). From a practical viewpoint, this means that two long-coated dogs bred together will produce only long-coated offspring. So if you don't want a short coat, but the dam of your favorite long coat stud is a short coat, don't worry; it will in no way affect the chances of you getting a short coat from such a breeding. On the other hand, if two shorthairs that were C/c were bred together, there would be a possibility that some (about 25 percent) of their offspring would be longhairs. If you don't want a long coat, you will need to look into the background more carefully, because you will have to play the odds by choosing a stud with the most remote long coat ancestors.

Health and Heredity

Most traits, whether physical or behavioral, are influenced both by genetic and environmental aspects.

83

Raising a puppy may require around-the-clock bottle feeding and care for weeks.

Because the hereditary aspects of many health and temperament problems are not always understood, it is best to take a cautious approach when contemplating breeding. There are too many wonderful healthy Chihuahuas available that can produce wonderful, healthy puppies; why take a chance with a less than healthy dam?

The mode of inheritance of patellar luxation, and of cleft palate are not known; but it is probably due to a number of genes acting together. The genet-ics of pulmonic stenosis and of cryptorchidism (def: undescended testicle[s]) are similar probably due to the combined action of several genes.

Hemophilia is inherited in the same way as it is in humans; that is, as a sex-linked recessive. This means that carrier dams pass it to half of their sons, who become affected, and half of their daughters, who become carriers; affected sires pass it to all of their daughters, who become carriers (except in the case where their dam, too, was a carrier, in which case a daughter could become affected), but to none of their sons.

Chihuahua Courtship

Make arrangements with the stud owner well before your female comes into season. Ask for a written contract that spells out what fees will be due and when, and what will happen if only one or no puppies are born. Both dogs to be bred should have a blood test for canine brucellosis, a primarily (but not exclusively) sexually transmitted disease with devastating effects on fertility. The female should also have a prebreeding checkup to ensure that she is in good health and does not have any abnormalities that would make whelping difficult.

Monitor her closely for signs of "heat" (estrus). These include swelling of the vulva and a red discharge, but in many Chihuahuas these signs may be subtle and go unnoticed. Most dogs are breedable for several days sometime between the eighth and eighteenth day of estrus, although earlier and later alliances have been known to result in pregnancy. Your veterinarian can also monitor your female's progress with vaginal smears or blood tests. As she approaches her receptive stage, she will tend to "flag" her tail, or cock it to the side when the male approaches or if you scratch around the base of her tail. Experienced stud dogs do not need calendars or microscopes!

Breeding dogs involves more than just letting a male and female loose together. Although this may seem like the natural way, in fact it is not natural for two dogs to breed when they may have just met each other. Neither dog knows the other well enough to trust its actions, so the female will often snap in fear when the male mounts, and the male may be dissuaded from mounting by her actions. Instead, after an initial period for introductions and flirting, the female should be held for the male. This is more easily accomplished if both dogs are put on a table (preferably against the wall in a corner, and on a rubber bath mat). If the male is smaller than the female, as is often the case with Chihuahuas, he may not be able to reach unless you provide him with a book on which to stand. With a reluctant female, the owner can support her under her hind legs with one hand; she can also be guided toward a male that might have bad aim, because attempts to guide the male will usually discourage him. Upon intromission the male will step from side to side, and then will want to jump off of the female and turn by lifting one hind leg over her back, so that they can stand rear to rear. This "tie" is perfectly normal for dogs and will typically last from 10 to 30 minutes. Keep both of them cool and calm during this time. If the male is much smaller than the female, he may have to be held in a higher position by his owner throughout the tie.

One day before delivery.

For optimal chances of conception, repeat the breeding every other day until the female will no longer accept the male. Be sure to keep her away from other males during this time; dogs are not known for their fidelity! The AKC will not recognize litters fathered by more than one sire.

HOW-TO:
Predicting Coat Color

One of the wonderful things about Chihuahuas is the rainbow of colors and patterns available. But this variability comes at the price of simplicity; still, most Chihuahua breeders feel it's worth it! The major differences from coat length genetics are that 1) instead of having only two alleles available for one gene, there may be as many as four (just remember, though, that any one dog can only have two of these four, one from its sire and one from its dam), and 2) there are several genes that may be interacting to affect the coat color, and in some cases an allele at one gene will actually mask the presence of an allele at another gene.

If you approach Chihuahua coat color genetics step by step, you will find that it's not really that difficult and worth the effort if you wish to make informed decisions about breeding for color. First look at your Chihuahua. What color is she? This is a harder question to answer than it may first appear to be. Ask these questions:

1. Is there any white at all on her? In Chihuahuas, there are four different alleles for different degrees of white spotting, with more white always recessive to less white. In decreasing order of dominance, the alleles at the **S** gene are:
• **S:** "Self-colored": dogs with no white. Because this is

caused by the most dominant allele, **S**, all such dogs must have at least one copy of **S**. But because **S** could mask any of the more recessive alleles, such dogs could be either **S/S**, **S/s^i**, **S/s^p**, or **S/s^w**.
• **s^i:** Next in dominance, this causes the so-called "irish-marked" pattern: white feet (and perhaps legs), tail tip, and collar. This is the pattern seen in Boston terriers. Such Chihuahuas could not have **S**, but could have one of three allele combinations: either **s^i/s^i**, **s^i/s^p**, or **s^i/s^w**.

A tan spotted dog...

• **s^p:** "Parti-color": predominantly white with patches of color. Such dogs can either be **s^p/s^p** or **s^p/s^w**.
• **s^w:** Mostly white, with a very few or no small patches of color. Because this is the most recessive allele, such dogs would need two copies of it: **s^w/s^w**.

If you want a solid-colored puppy, and you have a spotted female, you will never get one by breeding her to a spotted or even irish-marked male. Even if the parents of your dog, or of the stud dog, were solid colored, it

doesn't matter. You cannot get an **S** allele from spotted dogs.

2. You can think of the white areas on your Chihuahua as though a bucket of paint had been splashed over the dog, partially obscuring its "true" color beneath. Look beyond any white and see if you notice any pattern of black hair distribution. Black distribution is controlled by several alleles at two different gene locations, so sometimes they can interact and make things a little complicated. Now look at the influence of the two major gene locations one at a time. Those at the **A** location are a little easier to understand:
• **A:** Most dominant, results in a pure black dog. This is rarely seen in Chihuahuas.
• **a^y:** For most practical purposes, this is the most dominant allele of this series commonly seen in Chihuahuas. It produces a sable color, which is tan or

...plus a black-and-tan dog...

red with some black hairs interspersed throughout. Except for the possibility of some black hair on the ears, the dogs are basically a solid color. They could have the genotype of **a^y/a^y**, **a^y/a^s**, or **a^y/a^t**.

• **a^s:** Again rarely seen in Chihuahuas, this gene causes a black saddle on top of a tan body (such as the body color distribution of a typical beagle).

• **a^t:** The most recessive member, it is nonetheless not uncommon in Chihuahuas. This results in a black and tan pattern such as that seen in Doberman pinschers. Such dogs can only be **a^t/a^t**.

There have been people who have bred generations of black and tan Chihuahuas in hopes of getting pure black ones. If only they knew the genetics, they would have realized the futility of their efforts!

The other family of genes acting on black distribution is unfortunately a bit more difficult to understand. This is the **E** series, as follows:

• **E^m:** No matter what the pattern is from the **A** genes, this gene adds a black mask to it. In combination with **a^y**, it results in a sable dog with a black mask (such as is commonly seen in fawn pugs). With **a^t**, it would result in a black and tan dog with a sooty muzzle or dark face.

• **E:** Next in dominance, this results in no black mask.

• **e^{br}:** Rare in Chihuahuas, this results in brindle: irregular vertical black stripes running down the sides of the body over a tan background.

• **e:** Dogs with **e** will have no black hair anywhere, even if they are **A/A**, or **a^t/a^t**. It "overrides" the **A** gene in a manner of speaking. It is this allele, more than any other, that makes it difficult to make totally accurate predictions.

Now you have examined the pattern of white, which is due to the **S** family, and the pattern of black, which is due to the **A** and **E** families. What about the actual color, or hue, of the coat? Different aspects are controlled by different genes. An easy one is the **B** gene:

• **B:** Dominant; allows black pigment to be black. Most Chihuahuas have at least one copy of **B**.

• **b:** Recessive; makes all black pigment appear brown. In dogs that are **b/b**, or "chocolates," anywhere black is mentioned in this description of color genetics you can simply replace it by the word brown. So a dog that was **a^t/a^t** and **b/b** would be a chocolate and tan, rather than a black and tan. Chocolates also have brown noses and yellowish eyes.

Similar in action is the **D** family:

• **D:** Dominant; allows intense fully saturated colors.

• **d:** Recessive; makes all colors less saturated, and especially blacks more gray. These are known as "blue" Chihuahuas. Eye color also tends to be lighter.

Also similar is the **C** family:

• **C:** Allows intense fully saturated colors. Most Chihuahuas have at least one copy of **C**.

• **c^{ch}:** Decreases the tan coloration while allowing black to remain fully dark black. This creates a "chinchilla" color, sort of a mixture of gray and white hairs. Not common in Chihuahuas.

You don't have to have a computer mind with all of these allele combinations spinning around as you look at prospective studs. But if color is important to you, decide which aspects of color you care about. Many people find that playing with the possibilities are half the fun of planning a litter.

...could produce a litter having a wide variety of colors, including both parental colors, as well as black-and-tan spotted, chocolate and tan, irish marked, and solid tan, depending upon the recessive genes carried by the parents.

Lady in Waiting

Now you have two months to wait and plan. Gradually increase and change the expectant mother's food to a high-quality puppy food as time progresses. Keep her in shape, because a well-conditioned dog will have fewer problems whelping. At the end of the first month, your veterinarian may be able to feel the developing puppies, but this is not always accurate. Two encouraging signs of pregnancy that will appear at around this same time are a clear mucous discharge from the vagina and enlarged, pink nipples. If at any time the discharge is not clear, seek veterinary attention at once.

After the first month, avoid letting your pregnant Chihuahua jump from high places. When carrying her, be sure that you are not putting pressure on her abdomen. Do not give any medication without your veterinarian's advice. Your pregnant female should be isolated from strange dogs beginning three weeks before her due date; exposure to certain viruses during that time does not allow her to develop sufficient immunity to pass to her puppies, and can result in the loss of the litter.

Many females are prone to false pregnancies: a condition in which the breasts become slightly enlarged and may even have some milk. Pronounced cases involving large amounts of milk production, weight gain, and even nesting behavior and the adoption of certain toys as "babies" may be unhealthy and should be checked by your veterinarian. Some can be so convincing that even experienced breeders have thought their bitch was in whelp until she failed to deliver puppies!

You should be counting the days from the first breeding carefully. Be sure that everything is ready at least one week before the big event.

The delivery room: Where will the puppies be born? If you don't decide, you can be sure your mamma-to-be will choose your pillow! But her own whelping box in a warm, quiet room is really best. This whelping box will be her den and the puppies' home for the first few weeks of their lives. The sides should be high enough so that the young pups cannot get out, but low enough so that the mother can get over without scraping her now low-slung belly. In any case, the box should not be set directly on a cold floor, and should be lined with blank newspaper or preferably washable blankets. Newspaper has the disadvantage of being slippery for puppies just learning to walk; also, colored sections can contain harmful chemicals. If you use blankets, you must secure them on the sides so that there is no chance that a puppy could burrow under and then be crushed by the mother. You will find it much easier to assist in whelping if you place the box on a table for the process.

Talk to your veterinarian or an experienced Chihuahua breeder about what to expect at whelping. If possible, arrange to have someone on call in case of any difficulty. You will need the following: rectal thermometer, many towels and washcloths, nasal aspirator, dull scissors, dental floss, heating pad or heat lamp, and a warm box for placing newborns in while awaiting the arrival of any siblings. Keep a hospital atmosphere in your delivery room.

Several days before your long-coated Chihuahua's due date, clip the long hair from her belly, chest, and vulva. Then wash and thoroughly rinse these same areas in both coat varieties.

Labor day: Although 63 days is the average gestation time, there is some variability. Chihuahuas tend to be somewhat early rather than late. You can get about 12 hours of advance notice by monitoring the prospective

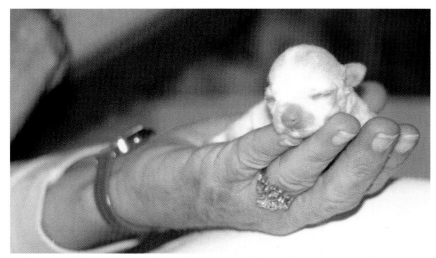

A 3.5-ounce (100 g) newborn fits easily in one hand. Typical birth weights are between 3 and 5 ounces (8.5–145 g)

mother's temperature starting around the fifty-sixth day; when her temperature drops to about 98°F (36.7°C), make plans to stay home because labor is soon to follow! Warm the whelping box to 80°F (26.7°C), and prepare for a long night. She will become more restless, refuse to eat, and repeatedly demand to go out. Make her as comfortable as possible and do not let her go outside alone where she might have a puppy.

As labor becomes more intense, she will scratch and bite at her bedding. The birth of puppies is messy, so at this point you should remove any blankets you wish to save. The puppies are preceded by a water bag; once this has burst, the first puppy should be born soon. As each baby is born, help the mother clear its face so it can breathe; then you may wish to tie off the umbilical cord about 0.75 inch (19 mm) from the puppy with dental floss, and then cut it. If you prefer, you can let the mother cut the cord, but watch to make sure she doesn't injure the pup. Her chewing action crushes the cord and prevents it from bleeding.

Each puppy should be followed by an afterbirth, which the dam will try to eat. Allow her to eat one, as they contain important hormones affecting milk production, but eating too many will give her diarrhea. You must count the placentas to make absolutely sure that none was retained in her; retained placentas can cause serious infection. Dry the puppy and place it on the mother's nipple to nurse. When she begins to strain to produce the next puppy, remove the first one to a safe box warmed to 90°F (32.2°C).

When to Call the Veterinarian

Cesarean sections should be scheduled for any dam under 4 pounds (1.8 kg); they may be needed in larger dams if:
• More than 24 hours have passed since her temperature dropped without the onset of contractions.
• More than two hours of intermittent contractions have passed without progressing to hard, forceful contractions.
• More than 30 minutes have passed of strong contractions without producing a puppy.

- More than 15 minutes have passed since part of a puppy protruded through the vulva and the puppy makes no progress.
- Large amounts of blood are passed during whelping. The normal color fluid is dark green to black.

Never allow a dam in trouble to continue unaided. It may mean her life.

Care of the Mother and Puppies

It is not always easy to tell when the last baby is born. If you have any doubts, have your veterinarian check the dam (you should bring her and the puppies for a post-birth check the next day anyway). Besides letting the mother and babies rest, your most important job now is to keep the babies warm. Puppies cannot regulate their body temperature, and chilling can quickly result in death. This is especially critical for small breeds. Newborn Chihuahua pups may weigh in at only 4 ounces (115 g). Whenever the dam must leave them, be sure that they are not in a draft. Use a heat lamp to maintain their environment at 85 to 90°F (29.4°C) for the first week, 80°F (26.7°C) for the second week, and 75°F (23.9°C) for the third and fourth weeks. Never feed a chilled puppy, except for a few drops of sugar water.

Watch the puppies as they nurse. Some pups must be helped onto the dam's nipples; some dams have nipples that are too large to fit in a pup's mouth. Pups with cleft palates will have milk bubbling out of their nostrils as they attempt to nurse. You should weigh each puppy daily on a gram scale to make sure that it is gaining weight. If not, ask your veterinarian about supplemental feeding. Some Chihuahuas may be hydrocephalic (suffering from an excess accumulation of fluid in the brain, which causes pressure on the brain and skull), but many are misdiagnosed with this condition by veterinarians who are not accustomed to the open fontanel typical of many Chihuahuas. If in doubt, find a veterinarian who has experience with Chihuahua puppies.

Chihuahua puppies are prone to hypoglycemia; if they appear disoriented or weak, give sugar water or honey and call your veterinarian.

Check to make sure that the dam's breasts do not become hard and swollen or painful, which could indicate mastitis. Although she will continue to have a bloody discharge for a week or two after the birth, any signs of infection or foul odor associated with it is cause for immediate concern. In cases of infections, mastitis, or eclampsia, you may have to wean the puppies early. By fitting the mother with a "body suit," such as a sock or sweater sleeve with four leg holes, she can stay with the pups without letting them nurse.

Chihuahuas, calcium, and eclampsia: Eclampsia is a life-threatening convulsive condition that may occur in late pregnancy or, more commonly, during lactation. It is more prevalent in small breeds and with large litters. The first signs are nervous panting, followed by vomiting and disorientation. Increasing muscular twitching and body temperature are definite danger signals. Convulsions are the last stage before death.

The condition seems to be brought about by a depletion of calcium. Many breeders of Chihuahuas used to supplement with calcium throughout the pregnancy in an attempt to ward off eclampsia, but it is now thought that such supplementation may actually promote eclampsia by interfering with the internal calcium-regulating mechanisms.

Once eclampsia does occur, the bitch must be taken immediately to the veterinarian for an injection of calcium and vitamin D in order to save her life. You may try giving calcium by mouth if she can swallow and if the trip to the veterinarian is long. *This is an emergency.*

Chihuahua Puppies

Chihuahua puppies are born with pink noses and eye rims that gradually turn dark beginning a few days after birth. The long coats can be told from the short coats because they will have a little ridge of longer hair down the nape of their necks. Dewclaws should be removed by three days of age (if at all). The puppies' eyes will open starting at around ten days of age, and their ears at around two weeks. This age marks the beginning of rapid mental and physical growth. They will attempt to walk at two weeks of age. Be sure to give them solid footing (*not* slippery newspaper!).

The dam will usually begin to wean her pups by four to six weeks of age; smaller pups may need to stay with her longer. At around three weeks, you can introduce the puppies to food: baby food or baby cereal or dry dog food mixed with water and put through the blender is a good starter. They may lick it off your finger or you may have to put their noses in it. No matter what technique you use, be prepared to declare the feeding arena a major disaster area by the time the meal is over. Puppies seem to think they can best eat with their feet!

Young puppies are irresistible, and your house may become the newest tourist attraction on the block. Don't let the puppies be overhandled, and don't allow the mother to become stressed by onlookers. Talk to your veterinarian about your puppies' vaccination schedule and visitors, because they could bring contagious diseases with them. After about six weeks of age, it is important that the puppies meet people so that they are well socialized, but this does not mean that they need to be exposed to a constant stream of new faces.

Locating the right new Chihuahua owner

Many experienced Chihuahua breeders are adamant that Chihuahua puppies should not go to their new homes until they are 12 weeks old, several weeks older than pups of most other breeds. Because the Chihuahua baby has little weight to spare, any undue stress or small illness could have serious consequences. An underweight puppy is best kept at home until it has built up some reserves, especially if being placed in an inexperienced home.

As the puppies get older and make progressively larger messes (and even little Chihuahuas can make huge messes), you may wonder whatever happened to your friends who were just dying to have one of Chiquita's babies. Now you may be faced with getting calls from strangers interested in buying these babies you've become so attached to. Remember the questions you asked yourself about whether a Chihuahua was the dog for you? You must ask these prospective owners how they plan to care for their puppy, what their long-term plans are for the puppy, and why they want a Chihuahua at all. One breeder relates that she evaluates prospective buyers by whether, if she had to give up the mother dog, she could be confident that this person would provide a good home for her. Chihuahua breeders do have one advantage over breeders of many other dogs: once a Chihuahua owner, always a Chihuahua owner. Do not be surprised if most of your inquiries come from people still grieving over the loss of their beloved former Chihuahua of many years.

But sometimes inquiries don't come your way. In desperation, you may be tempted to give your babies away. Don't. There are unethical people in the world who scour the classifieds for

An obviously proud dam.

free animals, and who have plans for these animals that don't include their surviving very long or living happy lives. People take better care of something in which they have an invest-ment, so don't cheapen your puppies' lives. It may take time, but you can find a good home. Of course, after a while it may become obvious that that good home you find is your own!

A healthy pup, ready to explore the world.

The Standard Chihuahua

What makes a Chihuahua a Chihuahua? Like every breed, the Chihuahua has a blueprint of the ideal specimen. No one dog ever fits that blueprint perfectly, but at the very least a Chihuahua should fit the standard well enough so that it is easily recognized as a Chihuahua. This possession of breed attributes is known as type, and is an important requirement of any purebred. A dog, even a lapdog, should also be built in such a way that it can go about its daily life with minimal exertion and absence of lameness. This equally important attribute is known as soundness. Add to these the attributes of good health and temperament, and you have the four cornerstones of the ideal Chihuahua.

The AKC Chihuahua Standard

General appearance: A graceful, alert, swift-moving little dog with saucy expression, compact, and with terrier-like qualities of temperament.

Size, proportion, substance: *Weight.* A well-balanced little dog not to exceed 6 pounds (2.7 kg). *Proportion.* The body is off-square; hence, slightly longer than when measured from point of shoulder to point of buttocks than height at the withers. Somewhat shorter bodies are preferred in males. *Disqualification.* Any dog over 6 pounds (2.7 kg) in weight.

Head: A well-rounded "apple-dome" skull, with or without molera. *Expression.* Saucy. *Eyes.* Full, but not protruding, balanced, set well apart; luminous dark or luminous ruby. (Light eyes in blond or white-colored dogs are permissible.) *Ears.* Large, erect-type ears, held more upright when alert, but

flaring to the sides at a 45-degree angle when in repose, giving breadth between the ears. *Muzzle.* Moderately short, slightly pointed. Cheeks and jaws are lean. *Nose.* Self-colored in blond types, or black. In moles, blues, and chocolates, they are self-colored. In blond types, a pink nose is permissible. *Bite.* Level or scissors. Overshot or undershot bite, or any distortion of the bite or jaw, should be penalized as a serious fault. *Disqualification.* Broken-down or cropped ears.

Neck, topline, body: *Neck.* Slightly arched, gracefully sloping into lean shoulders. *Topline.* Level. *Body.* Ribs rounded and well-sprung (but not too much "barrel-shaped"). *Tail.* Moderately long, carried sickle either up or out, or in a loop over the back, with the tip just touching the back. (Never tucked between the legs.) *Disqualifications.* Cropped tail, bobtail.

Forequarters: *Shoulders.* Lean, sloping into a slightly broadening support above straight forelegs that are set well under, giving a free play at the elbows. Shoulders should be well up, giving balance and soundness, sloping into a level back. (Never down nor low.) This gives a chestiness and strength of forequarters, yet not of the "bulldog" chest. *Feet.* A small, dainty, foot with toes well-split-up but not spread, pads cushioned. (Neither the hare nor the cat foot.) *Pasterns.* Fine.

Hindquarters: Muscular, with hocks well apart, neither out nor in, well-let-down, firm and sturdy. The feet are as in front.

Coat: On the smooth coats, the coat should be of soft texture, close and glossy. (Heavier coats with undercoats are permissible.) The coat should be placed well over the body with ruff on the neck preferred, and more scanty on the head and ears. Hair on the tail is preferred furry. In long coats, the coat should be of a soft texture, either flat or slightly curly, with undercoat preferred. *Ears.* Should be fringed. (Heavily fringed ears may be tipped slightly if due to the fringes and not to weak ear leather, never down.) *Tail.* Full and long (as a plume). Feathering on the feet and the legs, pants on the hind legs, and large ruff on the neck desired and preferred. *Disqualification.* In Long Coats, too thin coat that resembles bareness.

Color: *Any color.* Solid, marked, or splashed.

Gait: The Chihuahua should move swiftly with a firm, sturdy action, with good reach in the front equal to the drive from the rear. From the rear, the hocks remain parallel to each other, and the footfall of the rear legs follows directly behind that of the forelegs. The legs, both front and rear, will tend to converge slightly toward a central line of gravity as speed increases. The side view shows good, strong drive from the rear and plenty of reach in front, with the head carried high. The topline should remain firm and the backline level as the dog moves.

Temperament: Alert, with terrier-like qualities.

Disqualifications: Any dog over 6 pounds (2.7 kg) in weight. Broken-down or cropped ears. Cropped tail, bobtail. In long coats, too thin coat that resembles bareness.

A Champion Chihuahua?

How does your Chihuahua measure up to the standard? If you find yourself admiring your dog as it struts and poses around the house, you may be interested in showing off at a conformation show. At these shows, a judge will examine each dog from nose to

Some Useful Terms

Apple-dome: Top of the head is rounded in all directions.

Molera: Incomplete ossification of the skull.

Stop: Transition point from the forehead to the muzzle, as viewed in profile.

Scissors bite: The back surface of the top incisors meet the front surface of the bottom incisors when the mouth is closed.

Level bite: The tops of the incisors of both jaws touch when the mouth is closed.

Overshot: Incisors of the upper jaw project beyond those of the lower, leaving a gap.

Undershot: Incisors of the lower jaw project beyond those of the upper jaw.

Topline: The line from the neck to the tail, viewed in silhouette.

Sickle tail: Carried out and up in a semicircle.

Cat foot: Round, compact foot.

Harefoot: Long, narrow foot.

Hocks well-let-down: Hock joints close to the ground.

Reach: Length of forward stride taken by the forequarters.

Drive: Strong thrust from the hindquarters.

tail, feeling its body structure, studying its way of moving, and looking at the total picture it creates. Showing a dog can open an entire new world of exciting wins, crushing losses, eccentric friends, travel to exotic fairgrounds in remote cities, and endless opportunities to spend money. It is inexplicably addicting. As long as your Chihuahua has no disqualifying faults, you can show it—of course, you may not win, but you will still learn a lot about the show world and be better prepared in the event that you would like to show your next Chihuahua.

A lovely specimen of a smooth-coated Chihuahua.

A beautiful example of a long-coated Chihuahua.

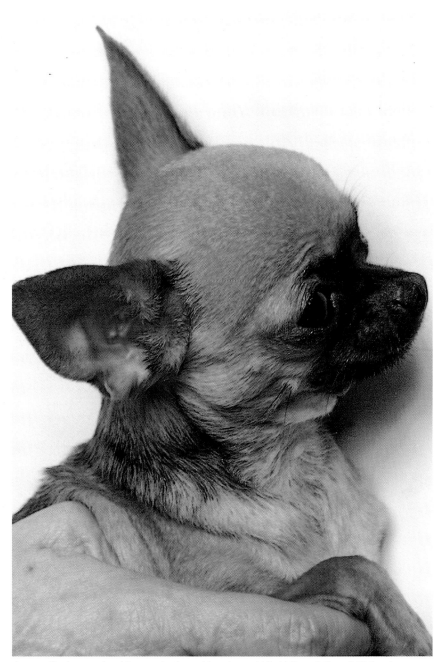

An excellent example of the apple-domed head sought in both varieties of Chihuahua.

Show Chihuahuas need to know how to pose on a table with all four paws pointing straight forward, legs parallel to each other and perpendicular to the ground, tail held high, head and ears up; they must also trot happily in a straight line by your left side. Most people use a tidbit to get the dog's attention in the ring. Some Chihuahuas tend to be overwhelmed by the hubbub of a dog show and will tremble and cringe. In fairness to your Chihuahua, you should take it to handling or obedience classes first to accustom it to being around other dogs.

Contact your local kennel or obedience club to find out if either has handling classes, or when the next match will be held. Matches are informal events where everybody is learning: puppies, handlers, even the judges. Before entering a real show, you should contact the AKC and ask for the dog show rule booklet. Your dog must be entered about three weeks before the show date, and you will need to get a premium list and entry form from the appropriate show super-

intendent (their addresses are available from the AKC or most dog magazines). Win or lose, never take one judge's opinion too seriously, and no matter how obviously feebleminded the judge is, be polite and keep your comments to yourself.

The two varieties of Chihuahua do not compete against each other; the dog chosen best Long coat as well as the one chosen best Smooth coat will go on to compete against the other Toy Group members for best Toy Dog. Only at shows held just for Chihuahuas does the best of each coat type ("Best of Variety") compete for the Best of Breed.

When at the show, you must be vigilant to ensure your tiny dog's safety when around other large dogs. Take your dog ringside in its small cage. Do not let your dog walk on the ground around large dogs, and even be cautious holding your dog in your arms around dogs that could jump up and bite it.

To survive as a conformation competitor, you must be able to separate your own ego and self-esteem from your dog; many people cannot do this. You must also not allow your dog's ability to win in the ring cloud your perception of your dog's true worth in its primary role: that of friend and companion. After all, your Chihuahua already knows it's a Champion, and will overlook any faults you might have.

Your Chihuahua never has to step foot in a show ring, earn a title, or thrill anyone except you to be the Chihuahua Champion of your heart. Whether sitting in your lap watching the world go by, protecting you from attacking leaves in the backyard, or doing any of the hundreds of things that make you wonder if your Chihuahua just might really be a human trapped in a dog's body, here's to many years of Chihuahua enchantment!

Chihuahuas posed for judging.

Useful Addresses and Literature

Clubs

American Kennel Club
   51 Madison Avenue
   New York, New York 10038
   212-696-8200

Chihuahua Club of America,
Inc.*
   Ms.Lynnie Bunten
   5019 Village Trail
   San Antonio, Texas 78218

Books

Gray, Thelma. *The Popular Chihuahua*. London: Popular Dogs Publishing Co., 1961.

Harmar, Hilary. *Chihuahua Guide*. London: The Pet Library, 1968.

Nicholas, Anna Katherine. *The Chihuahua*. Neptune City, New Jersey: T.F.H. Publications, 1988.

Riddle, Maxwell. *This is the Chihuahua*. Neptune City, New Jersey: T.F.H. Publications, 1959.

*This address may change with the election of new club officers. Contact the AKC for the current listing, as well as for the contacts for local Chihuahua clubs in your area and the Chihuahua rescue organization.

Terry, E. Ruth. *The New Chihuahua*. New York: Howell Book House, 1990.

Thurmer, Tressa E. *Pet Chihuahua*. Fond du Lac, Wisconsin: All Pets Books, 1962.

Watson, James, Anna B. Vinyard, Rosina Casslelli, Milo G. Denlinger, and Russell E. Kaufman. *The Complete Chihuahua*. New York: Howell Book House, 1978.

Periodicals

Los Chihuahuas
   12860 Thonotosassa Road
   Dover, Florida 33527

Dog World
   29 North Wacker Drive
   Chicago, Illinois 60606-3298

AKC Gazette
   51 Madison Avenue
   New York, New York 10038

TNT Toys
   8848 Beverly Hills
   Lakeland, FL 33809-1604

Dogs USA
   P.O. Box 6040
   Mission Viejo, California 92690

National Lost-Pet Registries

Tattoo-based Registries
National Dog Registry
   P.O. Box 118
   Woodstock, New York 12498-0116
   800-637-3647

Tattoo-A-Pet
   1625 Emmons Avenue
   Brooklyn, New York 11235
   800-TATTOOS (828-8667) or
   800-828-8007

I.D. PET
   74 Hoyt Street
   Darien, Connecticut 06820
   800-243-9147

Centralized Tattoo Registry Information
   15870 Allen Road
   Taylor, Michigan 48180
   313-285-6311

Microchip-based Registry
Info Pet Identifications Systems
   517 W. Travelers Trail
   Minneapolis, Minnesota 55337
   800-INFOPET (463-6738)

No Tattoo or Microchip Required
Petfinders
   368 High Street
   Athol, New York 12810
   800-223-4747

With visions of ribbons that are yet to be won, this youngster practices posing on a table as it will one day do in the show ring.

Sharing a tidbit and perhaps some pre-show strategy, these Chihuahuas and their owner demonstrate the confident and happy demeanors of potential winners.

Index

BARRON'S COMPLETE LINE OF DOG BREED OWNER'S MANUALS

Barron's *Complete Pet Owner's Manuals* include an extensive line of titles that provide basic information on individual canine breeds. The author of each manual is an experienced breeder, trainer, or vet. Each book is filled with full-color photos and instructive, high-quality line art. You'll learn what you need to know about each breed's traits, and get advice on purchasing, feeding, grooming, training, breeding, and keeping a healthy and happy dog.

Afghan Hounds
ISBN 0-7641-0225-7

Airedale Terriers
ISBN 0-7641-0307-5

Akitas
ISBN 0-7641-0075-0

Alaskan Malamutes
ISBN 0-7641-0018-1

American Eskimo Dogs
ISBN 0-8120-9198-1

American Pit Bull & Staffordshire Terriers
ISBN 0-8120-9200-7

Australian Cattle Dogs
ISBN 0-8120-9854-4

Basset Hounds
ISBN 0-8120-9737-8

Beagles
ISBN 0-8120-9017-9

Bernese and Other Mountain Dogs
ISBN 0-8120-9135-3

Bichon Frise
ISBN 0-8120-9465-4

Bloodhounds
ISBN 0-7641-0342-3

Border Collies
ISBN 0-8120-9801-3

Boston Terriers
ISBN 0-8120-1696-3

Boxers
ISBN 0-8120-9590-1

Brittanys
ISBN 0-7641-0448-9

Bulldogs
ISBN 0-8120-9309-7

Cavalier King Charles Spaniels
ISBN 0-7641-0227-3

Chihuahuas
ISBN 0-8120-9345-2

Chow Chows
ISBN 0-8120-3952-1

Cocker Spaniels
ISBN 0-8120-1478-2

Collies
ISBN 0-8120-1875-3

Dachshunds
ISBN 0-8120-1843-5

Dalmatians
ISBN 0-8120-4605-6

Doberman Pinschers
ISBN 0-8120-9015-2

Dogs
ISBN 0-8120-4822-9

English Springer Spaniels
ISBN 0-8120-1778-1

The German Shepherd Dog
ISBN 0-8120-9749-1

German Shorthaired Pointers
ISBN 0-7641-0316-4

Golden Retrievers
ISBN 0-8120-9019-5

Great Danes
ISBN 0-8120-1418-9

Greyhounds
ISBN 0-8120-9314-3

Huskies
ISBN 0-7641-0661-9

Irish Setters
ISBN 0-8120-4663-3

Jack Russell Terriers
ISBN 0-8120-9677-0

Keeshonden
ISBN 0-8120-1560-6

Labrador Retrievers
ISBN 0-8120-9018-7

Lhasa Apsos
ISBN 0-8120-3950-5

Maltese
ISBN 0-8120-9332-1

Miniature Pinschers
ISBN 0-8120-9346-1

Miniature Schnauzers
ISBN 0-8120-9739-4

Mutts
ISBN 0-8120-4126-7

Newfoundlands
ISBN 0-8120-9489-1

Pekingese
ISBN 0-8120-9676-2

Pomeranians
ISBN 0-8120-4670-6

Poodles
ISBN 0-8120-9738-6

Pugs
ISBN 0-8120-1824-9

Retrievers
ISBN 0-8120-9450-6

Rottweilers
ISBN 0-8120-4483-5

Saint Bernards
ISBN 0-7641-0288-5

Samoyeds
ISBN 0-7641-0175-7

Schipperkes
ISBN 0-7641-0337-7

Schnauzers
ISBN 0-8120-3949-1

Shar-Pei
ISBN 0-8120-4834-2

Shetland Sheepdogs
ISBN 0-8120-4264-6

Shih Tzus
ISBN 0-8120-4524-6

Siberian Huskies
ISBN 0-8120-4265-4

Small Dogs
ISBN 0-8120-1951-2

Spaniels
ISBN 0-8120-2424-9

Vizslas
ISBN 0-7641-0321-0

West Highland White Terriers
ISBN 0-8120-1950-4

Whippets
ISBN 0-7641-0312-1

Yorkshire Terriers
ISBN 0-8120-9750-5

Barron's Educational Series, Inc.

250 Wireless Blvd., Hauppauge, NY 11788 • To order toll-free: 1-800-645-3476
In Canada: Georgetown Book Warehouse • 34 Armstrong Ave.,
Georgetown, Ont. L7G 4R9 • Order toll-free in Canada: 1-800-247-7160
Or order from your favorite bookstore or pet store
Visit our web site at: www.barronseduc.com

(#110) 7/99

BARRON'S BOOKS FOR DOG OWNERS

Barron's offers a wonderful variety of books for dog owners and prospective owners, all written by experienced breeders, trainers, veterinarians, or qualified experts on canines. Most books are heavily illustrated with handsome color photos and instructive line art. They'll tell you facts you need to know, and give you advice on purchasing, feeding, grooming, training, and keeping a healthy pet.

Barron's Educational Series, Inc.
250 Wireless Blvd., Hauppauge, NY 11788 • To order toll-free: 1-800-645-3476
In Canada: Georgetown Book Warehouse • 34 Armstrong Ave., Georgetown, Ont. L7G 4R9
Order toll-free in Canada: 1-800-247-7160
Or order from your favorite bookstore or pet store
Visit our web site at: www.barronseduc.com

(#111) 7/99